Marriage and Divorce Hardships

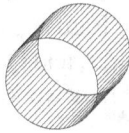

Author's Books

(As at 2016)

Non fiction

The Nature of Love and Relationships 2011, **2016** 2nd Edition
Doubts and Decisions for Living:
   Volume I: The Foundation of Human Thoughts **2014**
   Volume II: The Sanctity of Human Spirit **2014**
   Volume III: The Structure of Human Life **2014**
Relationship Facts, Trends, and Choices **2016**
The Mysteries of Life, Love, and Happiness **2016**
Marriage and Divorce Hardships **2016**
Gender Qualities, Quirks, and Quarrels **2016**
Relationship Needs, Framework, and Models **2016**

Fiction

Persian Moons 2007, **2016** 2nd Edition
Midnight Gate-opener 2011, **2016** 2nd Edition
My Lousy Life Stories **2014**

Love and Relationships Series
Inevitable Traps

Marriage

and Divorce

Hardships

Tom Omidi, Ph.D.

Love and Relationships Series # 3

Copyright © 2016 by Tom Omidi

Library and Archives Canada Cataloguing in Publication

Omidi, Tom, 1945-
Marriage and divorce hardships : inevitable traps
/ Tom Omidi.

(Love and relationships series ; 3)
ISBN 978-0-9938006-7-2 (paperback)

1. Marriage--Psychological aspects. 2. Man-woman
relationships. 3. Interpersonal relations. I. Title.

HQ801.O445 2016   306.8   C2016-902406-7

Published by Eros Books,
Vancouver, British Columbia
Canada

contact@erosbooks.net

Printed in the United States

Contents

Contents (Cont.)

List of Tables

INTRODUCTION

LIFE'S traps and sufferings are inevitable facts, as many dilemmas and conflicts challenge and distress us all our lives. Only the type, degree, and length of our pains differ, plus personal resilience and intelligence to handle them the best we can. We try to foresee and plan for possible social hurdles and learn to face them boldly, but destiny always holds the upper hand with a big sledgehammer hovering over our heads.

While nobody can elude life's hardships, causing so many of them ourselves in such high measures, especially in our relationships, reflects so much about our personalities and new culture. It reveals many depressing issues about humans' debility to think straight and relate to one another. It demonstrates our negligence for letting our lives, and life in general, get more out of control everyday in our supposedly modern societies. It shows that after so many millenniums of trial and error, we have not yet designed a satisfactory solution to live in society without hurting one another too much. Then we wonder why? Is it because humans are inherently incapable of relating, especially in marital relationships? Or, is it because we are not intelligent enough to figure out, or agree about, our relationship needs and objectives? Or, simply we are too stubborn and selfish to relate in a relationship despite our obsession to have a soul mate or at least a reliable companion.

Discussing life's dilemmas and humans' agonies requires many books. The goal here is to focus merely on human hardships and naïveté related to their marital relationships. Yet, this topic probably reveals a good bulk of our shortfalls that lead to personal and societal conundrums. To start, we should ask ourselves the following basic questions.

1. Do we know the **marriage purposes**?
2. Are we aware of **relationship challenges**?
3. What could be the **outcome of our oblivion** about a matter causing us so much personal hardships, not to mention all the ensuing chaos in society?

Marriage Purposes

The answer to the first question is a resounding 'NO.' We have lost track of our sense about this basic human need. We have not only lost our instincts about the purpose of companionship over the years, we have even eradicated that basic knowledge of 'marriage objectives' that religions and old cultures had injected in people's minds. Now, we are so horribly untrained and uncertain about marriage objectives. At the same time, we are quite adamant about what we must get out of our relationships according to our naïve and crooked views of individualism, equality, and greed.

In various group therapy sessions, divorced men and women were asked to mention the main reason for marrying their ex-spouses. The answers were quite informative. The typical answers were as follows:

- I loved him/her (the most popular answer)
- Mother/father figure
- Out of pity, I felt sorry for her/him
- Lifestyle change
- To stabilize my life
- To have a home

If we think about our own reasons for marrying, or when we ask others for their reasons, the answers are usually as obscure and surprising. They reveal the depth of our extremely low knowledge of marriage objectives. We marry for physical attraction, lust, biological clock, social/family pressure, finding happiness, psychological needs, misperceptions, love deficiency, financial issues, obsessions, security/insecurity, loneliness, or lack of any meaningful criteria to use.

If we ask others or ourselves about the success factors in relationships, the answer are again shallow and irrelevant for making relationships successful. At best, we might list some criteria, like love, security, longevity, communication, and wealth. Those with bad experiences in relationships are quite cynical about the possibility of building successful relationships, anyway. To them, relationships can be nothing but hell.

We have created our own subjective perceptions about the purpose and potentials of relationships based on our personal needs and superficial values around us. We have invented a fantasy in our heads about the nature of relationships and their success factors. Thus, we set ourselves up for failure, because our naïve expectations cannot be fulfilled. We (as a society) no longer have a common understanding of relationships and its purposes, let alone a grasp of the factors making them successful. Our educational systems, especially at senior high school, have failed to teach this essential subject to youths who need this knowledge so urgently. It is a pity that such an important matter, with such grave effect on social wellbeing, is left to personal interpretations instead of being researched and propagated for everybody's benefit.

Nevertheless, no one really knows relationship objectives or the parameters of a successful relationship nowadays. This ignorance is the result of rapid social changes that have tainted most people's personalities and their views of relationships. Accordingly, when the initial purpose of a relationship is not valid or solid, the chances of bringing objectivity into it would be slim. After a while, couples realize their mistakes and begin to resent their partners and themselves for being dragged into a relationship incapable of satisfying their needs, which are superficial most often anyway.

Accordingly, to deal with the existing chaos, we must show willingness and patience to learn about relationships' special needs. We must challenge our present mentality about relationships after studying the viability of people's rising personal needs and expectations from relationships in the new era. Then, we might start to view 'relationships' as a unique entity with specific needs. For sure, the process of acknowledging these needs and developing some principles for relationships would be gradual, because couples must learn to reduce their expectations from relationships and attend to their personal needs more independently. That would be a tough job but rather urgent.

A plausible list of relationship purposes are suggested and reviewed in Chapter One, due to their importance for the rest of the discussions in this book.

Relationship Challenges

The answer to the second question (on Page 2) is a resounding 'NO,' too. People have no grasp of relationships' needs and challenges due to the ambiguity of social structure, culture, values, and couples' high expectations from life and relationships. Couples have no idea what they are getting into and how to prepare themselves for those challenges proactively. They try to cope with a large variety of pressures and problems without knowing the real causes of the growing chaos in relationships. In fact, our modern society seems too relaxed or ignorant about the roots of pandemic marriage conundrums. We do not seem serious about facing the reality and admitting that fundamental changes and serious efforts are necessary. For one thing, we have not developed progressive mentalities and relationship models that can accommodate people's new lifestyles and needs. Ultimately, the question is whether we can still hope to infuse some objectivity back into our relationships, or do we wish to continue to feed, and live within, the rising relationship chaos? Another question is whether people's perceptions about life and their demands from relationships are realistic and useful, or only causing them more hardships in life merely due to their misplaced goals and priorities?

Naturally, our rampant social values are responsible for people's crooked mentality and lack of objectivity about relationships. On the other hand, our mentality and approach are further damaging the social structure and values. This vicious cycle is getting out of control, to what disastrous end, only God may know! Meanwhile, we face complex dilemmas and sad questions: Are we merely victims of low social morality, poor conscience, and a lack of direction? Are we now fully absorbed and hypnotized to the point of causing ourselves so much suffering without realizing the effect of our infected mentalities and the outcome of our present approach?

A vast amount of relationship challenges is overwhelming us, especially the new generations. They are discussed in this book along with a review of marriage purposes. Facing these challenges and bearing all the ensuing hardships of marriage and divorce are inevitable facts we have imposed upon ourselves out of our naïveté and arrogance. The question is whether there are solutions.

Outcome of Our Oblivion

The effects of relationship hardships on people and society are rather obvious to most of us. The repercussions of our naïve mentality about relationships are overwhelming us too. Thus, our oblivion to see the causes of all these pains feels quite baffling. Our reluctance to acknowledge the depth of relationship dilemmas we have imposed upon ourselves, as well as their personal and social ramifications, is rather shocking. In fact, our ignorance, indifference, or denial shows the depth of our social numbness.

The severity of relationship conundrums and challenges is evident in the depth of our misperceptions about relationships in the new era, as studied in the future chapters. For one thing, we usually imagine marriage as a happy occasion and experience. We have no idea about the agonies that marriage often adds to our already stressful lives. On top of its unique deep hardships, marriage also forces us into the very complex hassles of separation, divorce, and single parenthood. At the end, both our marriages and divorces are ruining our lives merely due to our indifference about the flaws of our present mentality and our raw assumptions about the potentials and purposes of relationships. We simply keep following the crowd within such a complex environment. It feels bizarre that we do this to ourselves so recklessly!

This book's goal is to address our responsibility in causing the rising personal and social instability, suggest some solutions to revamp our viewpoints, and perhaps seek better means of relating in our marriages—or at least evade this potential source of suffering by learning to live more independently. Instead of only bragging about independence, time has come to become self-reliant truly, which ironically teaches us the art of relating and depending on one another in a realistic manner as well.

PART I

Marriage

CHAPTER ONE
Relationship Purposes

THE following brief discussions of plausible relationship purposes are based on the author's studies and writings in his other books about love and relationships. Accordingly, the prevalent couples' expectations from marriage were studied and grouped into two categories: A) Sensible Expectations (purposes) that make sense for the new era, and B) Obscure Expectations (purposes) that are simply incompatible with modern lifestyles and people's obsession for individualism, equality, greed, pleasure, and happiness. Both groups of expectations, i.e., sensible and obscure ones, are reviewed in this chapter.

A. Sensible Relationship Purposes

Sensible relationship purposes are meaningful and useful for maintaining a healthy marriage in the new era, while partners value their independence and personal careers. They are:

1. Sex	2. Communication
3. Compassion	4. Companionship
5. Teamwork	6. MLove (tactful, adaptation love)
7. Friendship	8. Respect-Social acceptance
9. Personal Success	

Before reviewing the above general purposes in the following pages, it should be noted that the *ultimate objective* of relationships is to help couples face life's hardships together and reduce each other's burdens. Relationships could bring love and happiness to couples, too, but not as a main objective. The lack of adequate love or happiness is often only due to our exaggerated expectations from life and relationships as well as personal deficiencies. The reason for so many relationship failures nowadays is that our present mentality is unaligned with reality. We have no grasp of true relationship purposes, especially its ultimate objective of making life just a bit more endurable for partners. That is all! Strangely, most of us have never learned about the real purposes of relationships and instead trust our imagination and Ego to define some arbitrary notions. Thus, we often fail.

With the main objective of relationships in mind, we can contemplate other sensible purposes.

1. Sex: This is the most reasonable expectation from relationships. Since couples *attempt* not to look outside their relationships to fulfil this urge, they must depend on their relationships to satisfy this essential need. In fact, sex must be considered a basic purpose (or outcome) of relationships because partners' basic need for sex becomes ethically restricted, i.e., it becomes solely dependent upon their relationship; all based on the major assumption that relationships could and would satisfy this need. In reality, however, partners often withdraw sex as a tool for emotional blackmail or retaliation. In addition, sometimes partners cannot cooperate in this regard and thus look for sex elsewhere. Nevertheless, this is a legitimate objective for relationships. All other dramas surrounding sex cannot be helped either. Most of them are psychologically explainable and rather inevitable. The only advice is to learn about the role of sex more realistically instead of using it recklessly for blackmailing and hurting our partners.

2. Communication: Effective communication is obviously the essence of successful relationships, especially for enforcing teamwork. Thus, it is a major objective for relationships. However, many good relationships are ruined nowadays due to simple misperceptions and miscommunications. Partners' oversensitivity, arrogance, and false pride usually obstruct even their common dialogues. Effective communication is nowadays also essential for implementing a process of hassle-free separation when necessary. Instead of spending time and money on lawyers, a prenuptial contract, as well as partners' objectivity, can enhance communication when separation seems inevitable. Nonetheless, effective communication is the most difficult objective of relationships, because most often partners are not properly trained to communicate, or because retaliation and Ego make the process extremely hard to manage.

3. Compassion: Exchanging compassion is a logical purpose of relationships. However, in reality it seldom materializes at the desired level. This is because everybody seeks more compassion every day while the number of humble and patient people in society is shrinking. Therefore, it is wise to set our expectations rather low for receiving real compassion in relationships nowadays.

The problem is that we always crave sympathy, but have difficulty expressing it ourselves. Often we feel that our partners' needs are too superfluous and selfish. It is demanded too often or the nature of their expectations seems unreasonable to us. Therefore, the supply and demand for compassion are drastically unbalanced in societies and across the nations. Yet, instead of understanding this general shortfall of human nature, we take the matter personally and turn against our partners when they cannot give us as much compassion as we seek. We do not notice our own inability to offer genuine sympathy often enough, but we are needy for it so relentlessly.

On the one hand, couples should realize that expecting true sympathy is unrealistic in a modern society where the supply and demand for compassion are unbalanced—mostly due to inherent human nature. Stress and depression have simply made us vulnerable and too needy for sympathy, but there is nobody out there to give it to us.

On the other hand, compassion is a reasonable objective for relationships—with a major reservation in terms of its nature and source, since our realistic need for compassion cannot be fulfilled easily. Accordingly, a more realistic definition for compassion nowadays should mostly emphasize on our personal ability to generate it instead of craving it. The best way to achieve this is by becoming a better person and supplying more compassion to others than demanding it. We must realize that we should expect compassion only if we are good at generating it ourselves. Just needing something does not give us an entitlement to get it. The irony is that the more we learn to give compassion sincerely, the more we receive it from others naturally, and the less we feel the need for phony sympathies. By learning to become a compassionate person truly, we become self-sufficient largely and get a lot in return too. Therefore, in a sense, we can generate the compassion that we need personally. Only this mentality can reduce our depression and dependence on psychiatrists to manage our lives.

4. Companionship: This is an automatic outcome of relationships, but we do not quite know its purpose or the means of benefiting from this basic privilege of relationships.

We all prefer to have a companion, and relationships provide this chance, but the question is whether we prefer a lousy companion to loneliness. Conversely, finding an ideal companion is a matter of luck and usually a doomed expectation too. We all seek high quality companions to get love and compassion. A companion must be like this or that, we imagine, while we strive to satisfy our urge for love.

In all, we have no proper education about the purpose and process of companionship. Accordingly, our initial perceptions about companionship and our partner usually prove to be erroneous before long. Therefore, we alienate our partners quickly based on our past and present misperceptions, as well our inherent egoism.

The comments made before about the supply and demand for compassion and love, apply to companionship too.

5. Teamwork: An important purpose of relationships is to create synergy through teamwork. In addition, as we insist on more independence and individualism, the need for teamwork becomes greater in order to keep our Egos under a leash. Obviously, for teamwork, partners must have some genuine qualities, including modesty and objectivity. Yet, we nowadays face more *obsessions for individualism* instead of *modesty*. Therefore, finding partners of such quality and implementing teamwork in relationships would be a major challenge. Nonetheless, teamwork is an absolute purpose of relationships.

6. MLove: MLove (model love) refers to couples' tactful expressions of love to show compassion and social etiquette, and to relate smoothly. It will be argued in the next section (under Obscure Relationship Purposes) that love is not a real purpose of relationships. Instead, partners need some civilized and genuine *love attitude* toward each other in order to relate effectively. This narrow meaning of love (MLove) is, thus, a sensible purpose for relationships.

Many radical ideas have been proposed in this book. They make the nature of our relationships appear too dry and impersonal. This picture of pessimism might prove to be the reality that we must eventually face based on the values and the culture we are embracing so fast, most often inadvertently. Therefore, MLove is a helpful and relatively realistic expectation to induce passion in relationships. It reminds partners of the need to keep working on their relationship and communication.

7. Friendship: A good test of 'relationship success' is partners' ability to enhance their friendship. However, this idea has never been promoted as a relationship purpose. Often, couples actually prove their inability to be friends, but still insist naively to build a relationship. The main feature of successful friendships, which is missing in relationships, is that friends' limited expectations are set gradually and naturally without pressure or demand. Then even if those expectations are not fulfilled, they seldom argue or fight over them. They only moderate (realign) their own expectations to keep their friendship. They value their friendship so much they willingly reduce their expectations. This is indeed the strength of good friendships and a main reason for their success and longevity. This is exactly an opposite mentality we see in relationships. In relationships, couples set tough expectations immediately instead of appreciating the value of what they already have, like the way friends do. In fact, couples keep increasing their demands and expectations, and nag all the time, too, until their relationship falls apart. Therefore, a new purpose for relationship that should be promoted and analysed more actively is partners' aptitude for friendship. A relationship should be expected to be based more on friendship than love.

8. Respect/Social Acceptance: As part of our struggle for equality, independence, and identity, couples nowadays demand total respect from their partners. This is in line with social trends and thus an acceptable purpose for relationships. However, partners should not only expect respect. Rather, they should really learn how to respect their partners despite their obvious idiosyncrasies and personality weaknesses.

Society gives a higher status to family than individuals. We personally value our relationships highly for many reasons, too, but mainly because we expect them to help us fit better within the society. This is an automatic by-product and expectation from relationships.

9. Personal Success: A relationship should facilitate partners' personal success and independence. This seemingly selfish need of partners for personal success has a positive consequence for building their relationship, however. That is, with the emphasis on the personal success, partners need only look for the appropriate relationship model that can best fulfil the range of their personal needs. Otherwise, they should not even bother getting into a relationship. After all, if partners feel successful and fulfilled individually, their relationship would be a success too. It makes total sense.

Partners' cooperation is expected to give them a higher chance for success in social and personal endeavours. Synergy and moral support are the main objectives of companionship. In all, personal success is a reasonable and helpful criterion to include in the list of sensible relationship purposes. Unfortunately, in reality, the very sense of individualism and independence forces partners to compete with each other. Their unrelenting urges for recognition and showing off their independence and identity make them too arrogant at the cost of losing their relationship. Therefore, couples must not only choose the right relationship model based on their personalities and need for personal achievements, but also keep their Egos under a leash.

B. Obscure Relationship Purposes

Obscure relationship purposes refer to the wishful things we would like to have in our relationships, but do not happen normally. Therefore, we should not consider them as relationship objectives or requirements. We should learn not to fuss about them too much in order to make the best of all the other features of our relationships, as listed above under sensible relationship purposes. Every marriage can be successful without necessarily satisfying the obscure purposes discussed below. They might happen as fringe benefits of a good relationship, but not as a norm. Therefore, partners must build a proper mentality to never demand them from each other.

1. Dependence   2. Security
3. SLove   4. ELove
5. Trust   6. Happiness
7. Commitment   8. Longevity

1. Dependence: Partners' attempt to create a balance between their needs for both dependence and independence create a great deal of inner conflicts for them while complicating their relationship too. We get into relationships in most cases for relieving our loneliness. We need to depend on a partner to make our lives easier. However, in reality, many relationships make partners feel the ultimate sense of loneliness, especially psychologically. Relationships enhance our sense of loneliness many folds, because we feel the difficulty of relating to another person tangibly, and because we had imagined we could do all that rather easily, mostly on the power of love alone. Most of us had never felt so desperate and lonely psychologically when we were living alone. We are terribly disappointed after all those years of daydreaming about finding a partner to relieve our loneliness. Therefore, depending on our partners to cure our psychological loneliness is an unreasonable and obscure purpose to set for our relationships.

Another hurdle is that even if our partners were capable of satisfying our need for dependence, we personally sabotage their willingness by our constant expressions of individualism and independence. Our false pride prevents us from expressing our need for dependence and our partner's moral support directly. Instead, we pretend quite strongly to be emotionally self-reliant. Showing our neediness could tilt the balance of power in relationship, after all. Meanwhile, we strive to fulfil both our dependence and independence needs just by playing some superficial roles and expecting our partners to understand their meanings and also respond favourably. However, these conflicting (unexpressed) expectations and role-playing only frustrate our partners.

Since our emphasis nowadays is placed on individualism and independence, we must adjust our expectations from relationships accordingly. That is, **we should stick to independence and assume that relationships are no longer capable of satisfying our need for dependence at the desired level.** We must also prepare ourselves to deal with our inner conflicts (caused by inadequate dependence) without blaming our partners. Many readers might object: 'What is the point of being in a relationship if partners cannot depend on each other?' This valid question is answered in this and other books in this series. However, the bottom line is that we cannot really demand independence so strongly and also seek dependence. This does not make sense. Thus, dependence cannot be considered a legitimate relationship objective nowadays.

Of course, showing compassion always helps the health of relationships when couples notice their partners' need for dependence despite their arrogant show of independence. It is a good gesture by partners to stay civilized toward each other in those circumstances. That is why MLove is an important purpose of relationships—to make up for these irreconcilable dilemmas in relationships. However, when we keep switching between our independence and dependence urges and roles in relationships, we should also expect that our partners lose their sensitivity and true sympathy about our needs.

In our modern way of thinking, we accept open-mindedly that both dependence and independence are essential needs, and we naively believe we can cope with this major dilemma in our relationships. We might even assume that by some magical power we would find the right balance (between our needs for dependence and independence). We assume we can make compromises so that both partners can fulfil their rotating needs for independence and dependence by common sense. This is a highly obscure purpose to set for relationships.

Whether we like it or not, it is now time to adjust our assumptions about the conflicting needs of partners for both dependence and independence. It is time to stop the negative impact of these useless struggles on relationships. These facts should be clear to couples at the outset before getting married. This is necessary because, nowadays, the idea of 'dependence' has been losing its practicality in relationships. Therefore, couples must think through and plan their relationships based on the assumption that they must remain independent in all respects regardless of the outcome of their relationships. Hopefully, partners learn teamwork, MLove, and compromise, too, to make their relationships manageable. However, starting on the wrong foot, i.e., hoping that their need for dependency can be satisfied in a relationship, is simply opening the door for major disappointments.

2. Financial Security is a rather obsolete concept, although one partner is often the breadwinner in many relationships. The point is that financial security is no longer an automatic arrangement like the old times. People are not getting into relationships for financial security anymore. Or at least they should not when society is revolving around 'independence.' Now, financial security in relationships, when it happens, is mainly by accident or some kind of agreement between partners. It is an exception, not an expectation. Financial security is no longer a norm or a legitimate relationship objective, but rather a possible by-product of being in a relationship and only in the spirit of teamwork. Nowadays, partners should somehow understand and agree on the mechanism of their household finance before they commit themselves to a relationship.

3. SLove: Love can make couples' communication smoother and more effective. It also helps them satisfy their need for compassion. However, love does not qualify as a legitimate purpose for relationships, due to its illusive nature, especially SLove. SLove (selfless love) is the purest kind of love we feel toward our children, Nature, and possibly for our artistic creations.

We all like to taste love at least for starting a relationship, and love is a good gauge for measuring the degree of partners' attraction and success in satisfying their sexual need. However, we should not consider love a reliable factor to keep partners together. Love is not an objective measure for assessing relationships either. The reason is obvious. When we express love, we are influenced by a perception of Selfless love (SLove) while we are driven mostly by our Ego and love deficiency (ELove). We all have this spiritual need, SLove, to love someone or something passionately. When we meet a person who can stir this feeling in us, we consume ourselves with a perception of SLove. This individual becomes a mirage that satiates our need for SLove. At the same time, our need for ELove (ego-ridden deficiency love) further encourages us to identify this person as our soul mate. We are suddenly in love. This is great for bringing couples together. However, true SLove happens only rarely and only when partners are needless and enlightened persons. Therefore, our perception of SLove is only a transitory 'perception' and not a reality. ELove, on the other hand, is an absolute reality and not a perception. Therefore, ELove continues to place more demands on partners every day, because its only purpose is to feed partners' selfish need for attention. It creates possessiveness, jealousy, and frustration.

Overall, love, as we express it so readily nowadays, is not going to help relationships. Therefore, **we must remove love as a legitimate objective for relationships.** (Except for MLove.) We can use 'love' as a gauge for attraction and for facilitating communication, but not as a factor of relationship success.

The arguments presented before regarding 'compassion' apply here too. We all seek love too much but do not know how to give love. Again, the supply and demand for love (all three kinds, i.e., SLove, ELove, and MLove) are unbalanced and causing undue pressure on our lives and society in general. We have become too needy for love since everything else in society is stressful. And we assume that by stating love to someone, he/she gains the power or expertise to provide the genuine sympathy we need to mitigate social pressures.

4. ELove: (egotistic love) reflects the selfish need for love and attention and is mostly a reflection of insecurity. This type of love cannot be a legitimate purpose for relationships.

5. Trust: Unfortunately, mistrust is becoming a general condition in relationships nowadays. Therefore, trust cannot be a legitimate objective for relationships. However, partners should stop fussing about it and instead live with some level of suspicions and mistrust as long as the integrity of their relationship is not jeopardized.

6. Happiness: We expect relationships and our partners to bring us happiness. Yet, neither our partners nor our relationships are capable of providing happiness. Whether we can find happiness in relationships or not depends on a large number of factors, but mainly our mental capacity to interpret, absorb, and reflect happiness. In fact, relationship environments are normally too complex and demanding to exert direct happiness. Usually, if we are a happy person, we know how to generate our happiness within or without a relationship. The opposite is even truer. If we have no capacity for being happy, relationships normally make us unhappier. Therefore, in all cases, happiness cannot be a legitimate purpose to impose on our relationships or partners. They cannot be responsible for our happiness or the lack of it. Couples should accept that the only source of happiness that could be expected from relationships is the mere presence of a companion in their lives. If a partner's presence alone does not cause happiness automatically, then the relationship has no other source of happiness to offer. Under this circumstance, the couple must either learn to relate (at least passively) or opt for separation, but not nagging and demanding happiness.

Another misperception is to think that happiness is rather automatic in relationships because it can solve our personal problems. This is a false assumption and another illegitimate purpose to set for relationships in the new era. In fact, this mentality is destroying relationships and further reducing its capacity to cause even a slight measure of peace and comfort. As a whole, expecting relationships to solve our problems is a damned objective. A good relationship helps us mentally to deal with our personal problems more effectively, if we were smart and humble. A bad relationship, on the other hand, destroys our ability to even take care of our basic needs, let alone solve the complicated problems of life and the relationship itself. Judging by the statistics, more relationships fail than succeed in the new era. Therefore, instead of expecting relationships to solve our problems, we should expect and prepare ourselves to deal with the hardships of relationships, not to mention the high likelihood of separation. Relationships become the source of new problems instead of solving our existing problems. That is what this book, and the other books in this series are all about—trying to prepare the readers for the headaches of relationships.

Playing more roles and games to exert happiness would not work either. Although many experts advocate role-paying to make couples release their tensions and express the sources of their anxiety, this author believes that couples can decide about the viability of their relationships only by understanding the deep-rooted causes of relationship obstacles in the new era. Relying on the intelligence of partners to learn the sad truth about relationships works better than keeping them hopeful by playing some artificial roles. This is especially true when they are already under pressure mentally and physically. Role-playing causes more stress and frustration when partners feel the futility of their efforts deep down. Why they feel this way? From experience, we know that once the process of alienation between partners begins, it is almost impossible to return it to its initial state of moderate tranquility. The only thing that can save relationships is learning the truth about the real causes of problems, which often relate to partners' own irreparable idio-syncrasies.

7. Commitment: We have traditionally expected relationships to enforce some form of commitment for partners to stick to-gether even when some aspects of their relationship are not ideal. Maybe 'commitment' was a useful tool in the past and even now. However, as a practical step, partners must realize that nowadays the sense of commitment is vastly eroded by the need for individualism. Nowadays, couples insist on en-joying their lives at the highest level possible. They get out of their relationships sometimes even based on childish reasons or their perceptions of a better life with a different partner. The bottom line is that commitment can no longer be considered a legitimate purpose for relationships in the new era. Period.

8. Longevity: The above arguments used for 'commitment' applies to longevity too. It was a practical purpose in the past but not anymore. Points about Dependence and Teamwork also explain why longevity erodes due to people's inability to balance their rising needs for independence and dependence.

CHAPTER TWO
Marital Success Factors

WE can attempt to draw a list of success factors for relationships based on the discussions in Chapter One. We should, in fact, review both the sensible and obscure relationship purposes in that chapter in terms of their direct effects for the success of relationships. Hence, let us develop two lists based on the sensible and obscure objectives discussed in the last chapter: 1) a list of useful factors in line with the right purposes of relationships, and 2) A list of irrelevant factors and motives that preoccupy us and overwhelm our relationship decisions adversely. For making a stronger commitment, such as marriage (compared with the case of a simple cohabitation), we should be even less flexible and sloppy in terms of assessing the relevant and irrelevant success factors before choosing our partners. Relationship purposes and success factors are related concepts but not the same. We must know about, and expect, the right *purposes of relationships* and then work actively on *relevant success factors* to make our marriages flourish.

Relevant Success Factors for Marriage

Three relevant goals exist for marriage outside the instinctual needs to mate and have a family. They should exist simultaneously for making a positive decision about a particular marriage. These goals (motives) maximize the interests and welfare of two intelligent individuals who view marriage as an institution or partnership. These three goals (marriage success factors) are explained in general here and then their elements are elaborated in detail in the next chapter.

Increase Life Enjoyment: Marriage provides the opportunity to explore life jointly in a more significant manner. Obviously, sex, love, and compassion are expected to prevail and provide enjoyment, especially during the early stages of our lives when we need all those good things the most. However, sharing experiences in general and doing certain activities together intensifies partners' enjoyment of life extensively as well. Life's inherent values become more vivid and meaningful when they are explored and appreciated jointly, while partners express their feelings and interpretations. Just the mere opportunity to have someone around to discuss, or complain about, life and social issues gives couples a warm sense of relief if not enjoyment. Married individuals have a longer life expectancy, mostly because they can share their joys and anguish. They get a chance to share their hurts, mitigate the effects of external pressures on them, and get back into happy mood cycles faster.

Support and Cooperation: Marriage should provide a suitable environment for cooperation and teamwork to solve problems, and to strive for higher personal achievements. Partners' joint participation in household and family affairs leads to better results and a higher synergy with less energy wasted by each partner. More importantly, partners are expected to support each other functionally and psychologically in order to grow, think clearer, and stimulate a variety of communications that would be creative and thought provoking.

Sensible Commitment: The ultimate purpose of marriage is companionship. However, while 'companionship' remains a romantic and natural notion, 'marriage' comes across as a contractual obligation of partners for a joint venture. We do not think and feel as much romance when we talk about marriage as it is inherent in the meaning and purpose of companionship. This subtle expectation of romance fading with marriage is, of course, a realistic vision based on what we subconsciously know and observe in most marriages. Our negative direct experiences and general observations in society have created a dubious perception about marriage. It appears, particularly, that men are more reluctant to commit themselves to marriage, partially to protect their independence and partially due to their higher apprehension about married life and its inevitable anguish—perhaps because they have less maternal incentives that goad women more naturally and forcefully.

It seems as if with marriage we expect the innate purpose of companionship lose its steam eventually in spite of partners' unparalleled initial love and romanticism. Accordingly, marriage seems more like a scheme to keep partners together even under situations not tolerated in a non-committal companionship. Although we are not naive to assume that problems of alienation can be resolved by making separation difficult through marriage arrangement, we believe that some simple formalities (like the ones we now have) can protect us from the situations where our agitated Egos explode and we make hasty and regrettable decisions. Through marriage, we are forced to learn and practice some common sense in making our relationships work instead of searching for an ideal mate forever. After all, ideal couples can be found only in fairy tales. Nowadays, however, couples are unaware of, or ignore, even this basic purpose of marriage, i.e., a sensible commitment.

In marriage, we may eventually learn that stubbornness and false pride only lead to alienation and separation. We expect the loss of some intensity and passion in companionship over time, but hope to acquire the wisdom of comradeship to accept and adjust to our partners' imperfections. These same imperfections would have separated partners if they were not married, and had not learned the means of overcoming their stubbornness and false pride.

Therefore, marriage has a special purpose that makes it distinct from a simple companionship. We may call this a 'sensible commitment' to make a relationship work if it is logically possible. However, most of us are not acquainted with this basic purpose of marriage, or do not work on it consciously as a major requirement of marriage. Contrary to full commitment that many naïve partners dream and expect from their marriages, 'sensible commitment' is conditional upon partners' ability to relate in many respects *in order to develop* a natural sense of commitment when hardships or conflicts arise. The sensible commitment grows naturally when partners learn to relate peacefully and respectfully, instead of expecting a blind commitment egotistically. Our view and concept of marriage is an incomplete picture, which we have learned from our parents and movies. We have never had an opportunity to understand the real purposes (and shortcomings) of marriage before we get into one. And once we are in it, we do not know how to assess and respond to complex situations prevalent in modern relationships. We either suffer through it too much too long helplessly or run away from it prematurely, based on our emotional and arbitrary criteria for tolerance.

Irrelevant Success Factors for Marriage

The most commonly misperceived success factors for marriage or a serious relationship in the new era are:

Love Need: This is a strong and beautiful need that we crave permanently, but often at the expense of a lifetime misery and disappointment. Everybody is misled by mushy movies that show how love makes people's life eternally beautiful and happy. 'Love need' occurs in three ways and waves. First, we crave being loved per se, like a psychological deficiency. Second, we imagine and believe that we adore a particular person and cannot live without him/her. Third, we superficially build an image of love in response to the sentiments that we believe a person is offering us, which we usually accept out of loneliness, desperation, or our innate urge to love or be loved—and thus we replicate the feeling of love. None of these love criteria is directly relevant for building a serious relationship.

Therefore, while we are trained to believe love is the main factor for the success of relationships, we must now turn 180 degrees and accept that it is not—just to focus on true success factors.

Security and Dependence: The traditional assumption about the capacity of relationships to full our needs for security and dependence is no longer valid in the new era. We should no longer gauge the value of our marriages based on the level of security and dependence it can provide. They are good features to have in relationships, but their absence should not reflect on the viability and success of relationships. These factors, security and independence, are against the basic principle of self-reliance and self-image that we value so much nowadays. Starting a partnership in a weak position would not help the relationship in the long run. Insecurity puts demands on both partners. The spouse who requires special attention and a sense of security would most likely be disappointed after marriage to find out that his/her spouse does not care or cannot provide the extreme attention that is demanded of him/her. The spouse pressed for special attention eventually gets fed up with his/her partner's abnormal demand and withdrawals from the relationship.

The success of relationships nowadays depends largely on the personal strength of partners and their abilities to increase synergy in their relationship, instead of being a needy individual.

Financial Gain: It is needless to discuss the immorality and irrationality of planning personal gains as a factor of success in a marriage or companionship. Yet, many partners bring their calculating nature to relationships nowadays.

Convenience: One or both partners consider marriage a means or matter of convenience, financially or emotionally. Sometimes they do it just for changing their monotonous life routines. Family and cultural pressures to build a family often lead to these types of marriages too. Marriage is used as a scapegoat, while partners remain oblivious of its enormous potential for causing major headaches, frustration, and inconveniences of its own, instead of solving their initial problems. Focusing on personal problems and inconveniences, which partners hope to eliminate through marriage, often reflects their ignorance of relationships' peculiar needs and capacity.

Now that we are familiar with the relevant and irrelevant success factors for relationships, the next challenge is to find means of pinpointing and measuring them when we meet a prospective partner. Now we can study the details of the relevant success factors in the next chapter, while we eliminate the irrelevant factors from our minds. In fact, the whole purpose for setting and measuring couples' compatibility should be to gauge the favourability of relationship success factors. Merely checking partners' compatibility in terms of sharing some traits—as is common nowadays—does not guarantee that their relationship would be successful. Instead, we must measure each partner's ability to focus on, and practice, particular success factors in order to enrich his or her marital relationship.

CHAPTER THREE
Couples' Compatibility

PARTNERS' personality attributes and their capacity for fulfilling the three marriage purposes (i.e., increase life enjoyment, support and cooperation, and sensible commitment) can provide a relative measure of their compatibility. By assessing these success factors, we can estimate two people's ability to relate without inflicting too much harm on each other. Overall, however, finding compatible partners is becoming more difficult every year due to the rising complexity of personalities and social values, and also due to partners' ignorance about the real success factors in relationships in the new era. Instead, they only put more demands on each other and raise their expectations from their relationships.

Compatibility to Increase Life Enjoyments

An implied expectation, when two individuals join, is to create synergy in all respects, including an enhancement in their life enjoyments above the levels that partners can attain personally. If partners cannot deliver what is needed to achieve this added mutual enjoyment, the purpose of marriage becomes questionable. Partners begin to doubt the value of staying in such a lousy relationship. So let us discuss a few main factors that contribute to partners' increased life enjoyments.

Physical Attraction

Physical attraction brings two individuals together quickly and provides a great foundation for building all other aspects of a joint life. It simply reflects our needs for sex, love, and companionship, without the extreme implications of being in love or being desperate for it. In the context used here, physical attraction is the positive feeling we sense for being close to our partner, both physically and mentally. It is an authentic sense of connection and friendship between partners, rather than a flimsy infatuation. Yet, this general attraction helps partners satisfy each other's need for love and sex naturally. It also motivates partners to learn patience and tolerance, whereas without such attraction they would feel trapped or leave each other with the smallest disappointment.

Communication and Negotiation Abilities

The compatibility of partners' personal values and philosophy of life is important for increasing their life enjoyment, but their ability to communicate their viewpoints effectively is even more essential for increasing their life enjoyments. They should be flexible, articulate, and patient, instead of dogmatic, opinionated, and hyperactive. They must be able to express their feelings and needs calmly without getting into quarrels, or withdrawing quickly because their communication feels futile or frustrating, e.g., when they fail to manipulate their partner perhaps. In all, a major test of compatibility is to find out how intelligently and calmly two partners can discuss various issues. Ability to negotiate and be assertive is important for keeping the communication channels open and productive. Conversely, emotional reactions prevent partners from ever finding their common interests even when there may be some. Without proper communication, finding common grounds for exploring other compatibilities and sharing life enjoyments gets difficult. It would feel as if partners are totally incompatible when in fact both partners might have high qualities.

Communication is an important factor for increasing partners' life enjoyments because it plays a wide range of roles for team playing, relating, sharing experiences, etc. The quality of communication is rather easy to measure, fortunately, if we look for the right clues actively.

Most communication problems arise when one partner becomes the sole (or main) communicator prior to marriage. Partner 'B' agrees with, or simply absorbs, whatever 'A' says without expressing enough personal opinions. Thus, 'A' believes 'B' is in agreement with him/her and his/her viewpoints, which gratifies A's egoism and sense of control. In reality, though, this is merely a sign of potential problems waiting for future explosions.

Partner B's seeming passivity may have several reasons. S/he may disagree with everything or most of what 'A' says, but holds back his/her comments because s/he does not want to contradict 'A' and jeopardize their relationship. Or s/he might be dominated by 'A' and does not *yet* know how to correct the situation and be assertive. Or, s/he does not have any special ideas or thoughts to contribute to their communication, and thus s/he is simply content with this one way communication, at least for now. Thus, incomplete, stressful communication prevails between partners.

Then, after marriage, the (passive/aggressive) 'B' makes his/her abrupt entrance with a new tactic as a very active/ aggressive partner. S/he makes her voice heard, which in most cases would be aggressive to make up for all the past inhibitions, and also because s/he does not know a better method of communicating. Even if there were a slim chance that 'B' does not rebel, 'A' would eventually feel the void and the lack of some intellectual communication with his/her partner, especially when his/her attempts to communicate are blocked by passive aggression and retaliation. An Ego dominated partner

(maybe 'A') usually dominates their communication and relationship too much. Conversely, a Model (maybe 'B') tries to
accommodate his/her partner by agreeing with his/her viewpoints and even encouraging his/her way of thinking. Eventually, however, both partners feel dissatisfied with this meaningless way of communication and its results. Especially,
Model (maybe 'B') who only listens in the first phase usually
rebels or withdraws eventually, leaving 'A' completely in
shock and rejected.

Life enjoyments stem from good communication and exchange of valuable thoughts. If partners are incapable of stir-
ring each other's thoughts, they eventually look for it elsewhere. Therefore, prospective marriage partners must know
what real communication entails and ensure that theirs is en-
riching and compatible at their intelligence levels. Partners
need good communication skills in order to relate effectively.
Yet, a more important role of communication is to increase
partners' enjoyment in life.

We can test our communication abilities easily. If communication is dominated by one side, if partners always end up
fighting and withdrawing, if one or both partners are not able
or willing to express themselves and are secretive or ignorant,
or if a partner is deliberately only a listener, then there is a
great likelihood that there would never be a reliable and
healthy communication between partners. Communication is
obviously the main cause of relationship failures, due to its
essential role for cooperation, relating, sharing experiences,
and increasing partners' life enjoyments, etc.

A sign of a good communication is that partners equally
and enthusiastically share their thoughts, get into arguments
without ending in fights or withdrawals, find ways of compromising from time to time, and know how to negotiate for
achieving satisfactory and productive results. They look for
win-win solutions instead of being competitive. There would
probably be some occasional fights and temporary withdraw-

als between these couples too, but the frequency is negligible compared to those couples who almost always get into trouble every time they attempt to communicate, or nothing comes out of their communication.

Activities and Thoughts to Share

Without compatibility in lifestyle and thoughts, marriage would be a never-ending cycle of burning rage and freezing apathy—fights and withdrawals. Partners should have common thoughts to share regularly, especially on personal topics such as hobbies, self-awareness, life values and philosophy, social and political issues, etc. They should enjoy their discussions per se, rather than doing it randomly merely out of necessity, mostly for solving problems.

While enhancing their life enjoyments through sharing of their *thoughts*, partners must also share certain activities and seek ways of appreciating the aesthetic values of life and Nature. If they do not have compatibility in *things* they like, and like to do, at best they end up doing mostly their own things, while missing the joy of sharing activities and thoughts, as inherent human needs.

Some people have peculiar needs that reduce their chance of compatibility with others. For an artist who finds special values in art and Nature, for example, living with a partner who is indifferent about these experiences would be tough and lonesome, especially if his/her partner does not have enough things to do him/herself, which would then often lead to more nagging. Of course, partners need not appreciate everything equally all the time as long as they have enough thoughts to share and things to do together without partners losing their independence or feeling pressured for attention.

Many couples get into serious quarrels because of their perceptions about inadequate attention, differences in tastes about food, the house they like to buy, outdoor activities, common friends, and other basic things that nobody could have

have imagined would cause so much friction after marriage. Obviously, partners would never agree on everything. That is why an effective communication is necessary to discuss their opinions and differences calmly. With good communication, some of their conflicts due to inadequate attention or common activities can be resolved. They learn to make the best of their times together for sharing at least some thoughts and activities, while they give each other ample room for independence.

One way of testing and measuring this compatibility is to prepare a list of major interests and activities that partners like to do alone or share together, without trying to influence, judge, or ridicule each other's tastes and preferences. Of course, some of these interests should have become obvious during the initial courtship without a need to prepare a list. However, making a list indicates the seriousness of the activities and interests as part of their life plans and not only during a short period. The list must contain only the items they regularly do and are sincere about, and not their dreams. Simple things, like a stroll in Nature, athletic endeavours, artistic explorations, reading and discussing a book, and gardening are some good factors for measuring partners' compatibility. Then, they can sit back and decide how they can satisfy those needs (their own and their partner's), without compromising too much just to make their partner happy. And they should definitely stop assuming they can gradually make their partner understand and enjoy sharing the same activities.

Thus, the first set of compatibility factors (for increasing life enjoyments) consists of, i) physical attraction, ii) communication method and content, and iii) major thoughts and activities that partners can share. Together, these factors enhance their life enjoyments.

Compatibility for Support and Cooperation

The second group of compatibility factors contains the elements of support and cooperation in 'family,' which requires partners' goodwill and conscious efforts. Obviously, couples have the intention of cooperating and supporting each other in order to achieve common family objectives as well as their personal goals. However, they hardly know how to go about doing it.

Everybody has some vague ideas about marital obligations and duties. However, support and cooperation is much broader than obligations and responsibilities, which have by the way lost their meanings in marriages nowadays, anyway. Our needs for individualism and equality have eradicated all those good family values (i.e., obligations and responsibilities) that prevailed in old cultures. Therefore, partners must now measure, at the outset, their own and their partner's compatibility factors for support and cooperation, e.g., one's capacity for compassion and teamwork, instead of depending on their implied intentions and promises.

Creating children is still the most basic and natural intention (rightly or wrongly!) for building a family, and it is our only creation with such complexity in physical and mental capabilities and a soul too. This exalting creation that we so casually view as our common objective in marriage is built in response to our instinctual need and understanding of cooperation and support. Without a mutually strong sense of compassion, cooperation, and support, even this basic objective remains invalid and cannot bear fruit. Raising a healthy kid requires smart parents. We have similar instinctual needs to exchange compassion, support, and cooperation with someone we trust in order to achieve and share better things in life. Partners must be able to look up to each other to play their roles effectively in their marital relationship.

Some of the factors related to this category of compatibility are discussed in the following pages.

Teamwork

Partners' ability for teamwork is the first criterion (factor) to measure for 'support and cooperation' compatibility. Teamwork deficiency is not merely a symptom of personal negligence, but rather bad universal training. Nowadays, the market economy and competition influences our mentality and attitudes too much. The important lesson we learn at home, at school, and in society is to compete and win in order to prove our identity. Our value as a person is mostly determined by our superiority over others. In professional sports, physical ability and competitiveness leads to outrageous levels of compensation. Our children want to be like so and so basketball or hockey player in order to be rich. The sense of competition defines the whole purpose and structure of organizations. In our jobs, we get involved with ruthless strategies to defeat our company's competitors, and we get into competition with our colleagues and bosses, too, to acquire higher positions and money. Competition is evident and encouraged in everything we do. We are sacrificing our compassion for competition. This mentality is not restricted to social and economic settings. Family life has become equally contaminated by this evil as well.

Instead of teamwork, marriage partners nowadays appear more and more in competition with each other in all respects. They compete at home with the same tactics and personality aspects they apply for outside competition. They compete to acquire the power and status in family, as if it were another heartless entity to capture and control. Another factor hindering teamwork is people's obsession nowadays to gain and stress their 'individualism,' without really knowing its true meaning. They perceive it as a way of becoming more selfish and assertive.

Marriage partners fight to strengthen their positions and enforce their viewpoints. They struggle to dominate the situations and each other. They compete for the love and respect of their children. They struggle to implement their own ways and theories with kids. They compete by trying to prove they work harder, deserve more, are more hurt, make more money, are right, know more, etc. Thus, their simplest disagreement turns into endless quarrels, retaliations, or desperate submission of one partner. Children learn who runs the household and who has the ultimate power to set the direction of their lives and overrule their whims.

Overall, despite widespread propagandas in organizations and society, teamwork has found very little application in our lives. The pretences and talks of teamwork may deceive us to think that perhaps we can finally tame our dogged Egos and harmonize our intentions regardless of our personal interests. Alas, the competition, as the core of our social values, has inflicted our family life and is preventing teamwork to prevail. Competition is destroying the sense of trust that teamwork requires. Yet, partners need teamwork for supporting each other and for propagating proper family values and wishes. As long as partners place personal goals ahead of family objectives, there would never be a chance for compatibility in support and cooperation.

Like most other personal deficiencies, the sense of competition and control in family life emerges at different degrees. We can try to measure the intensity of our companion's competitiveness and domineering attitude rather than expecting to find an absolute team player. We can measure our partner's teamwork capacity from his/her reaction to losing in a game; or when s/he has a choice between collaboration and competition. We can design situations and games to learn about our partner's egoism turning into rivalry in everything s/he does. Then, we can take the same tests ourselves and determine how good a team player we are!

We fail to create a teamwork attitude and environment also because we always insist on being *right* about everything, and to prove our partner *wrong*. We must have the last word about everything and we are certain we know the best for everybody. This attitude becomes mostly evident after marriage when partners feel less obliged to impress each other by humble and gentle behaviour. Just to use an anecdote, whenever an occasion came up, a couple (J. and M.) used to joke sarcastically about a global reality, perhaps in a somewhat exaggerated tone for fun. J. pointed out that prior to their marriage, M. kept saying, "You are right" about all the comments and suggestions J. made. But the next day after marriage, the first comment J. made, M. told J., "You are wrong." Regardless of the truth that J. and M. were sharing with their friends for fun, the anecdote reflects the gist of dramatic change in relationships after marriage.

Partners should discuss their 'common' goals and find out how they are planning to go about them and what those goals really mean behind the surface.

Support of Personal Goals

Teamwork is essential for achieving common goals, including household activities. However, individual goals of partners should also receive high attention in a relationship. Partners should demonstrate their interest and ability to support each other in pursuing their life objectives. Initially, it is important that partners know their major personal objectives in life and discuss them together seriously. The intention is to evaluate each other's true feelings and reactions about their goals, which are usually left out in casual conversations. When our personal aspirations are discussed a few times, especially if we are already pursuing those goals, the true reaction and the potential for support can be witnessed and assessed. However, it is crucial to have real personal objectives rather than faking ideas (dreams) that partners are not serious about. We always think of new ideas and goals after marriage, too, which can be discussed as they develop to show our general interest to receive our partner's support too. The point is to discuss our personal plans when we feel serious about them.

Frequently, a partner has a vague idea, or perhaps even a strong desire, to pursue some special goal and mention it casually. Then, s/he neglects to pursue her/his plans because of his/her lack of motivation, perseverance, ability, or any other personal shortfall. Yet, s/he uses marriage as an excuse, or blames his/her partner, for not pursuing his/her goals. S/he eventually believes in this injustice even him/herself and becomes convinced that marriage and/or his/her partner had been the cause of his/her failure. Many family frictions arise because partners forget to discuss their personal objectives seriously, but mention all kinds of lost dreams because of marriage. Usually when a partner does not have personal goals in life, s/he holds the other party responsible for his/her perceived or real failures. However, partners should realize that if they allow marriage stop them from pursuing their goals, they have only themselves to blame. If we do not envision our personal aspirations seriously before marriage or do not get the motivation to pursue them after marriage, our partner should not be used as a scapegoat. If we make mistakes, or get caught in unpleasant situations contrary to our plans, we must blame our destiny or personal negligence, but making false claims or blaming our partner for our failures only reflects our poor character and immaturity.

Another cautionary point is that if a partner has lower or different aspirations in life, s/he would often *try* hard to bring down the aspirations of his/her partner equally to the same level as his/hers, instead of making an effort to catch up with him/her. One partner's lack of life philosophy or aspirations affects the lives of both adversely. Similarly troublesome would be when one partner's life philosophy and aspirations are outside the popular social norms.

Psychological Support

Partners must assess each other's patience and compassion to support their personal objectives before making the marriage decision. Moreover, they should measure their capacity to provide mental and psychological support in general for small and major issues. This kind of support helps relieve the stress of daily work and life challenges. It also stimulates communication and strengthens the scope of relationship.

Problem Identifying and Solving

Along with partners' ability to communicate, they should also be good in joint problem identifying and solving. This requires mutual understanding of each other's analytical approach and use of logic in assessing and addressing the situations and issues, finding practical solutions, and making rational compromises. Testing this ability is not difficult either. A hypothetical family problem or any story from the news can be raised along with some personal suggestions for a solution. We then wait for our partner's participation and suggestions for solving the problem at hand. We can assess the process after a few typical discussion sessions.

The second set of compatibilities that we should seek in our prospective marriage partner consists of: i) Teamwork for common objectives, ii) support to pursue personal goals, iii) ability to provide mental and psychological support, and iv) joint problem solving capabilities. Together these four factors create an environment of cooperation and support to nurture a friendly and constructive relationship.

Compatibility for Establishing a Sensible Commitment

History and experience clearly show that all the promises and vows we make at the wedding and all the good intentions we have when we join with our partner in matrimony are worthless. When a couple is not compatible, life often becomes hell for them. Hence breaking their promises and commitments becomes the most natural and viable option for them. Some particular personal traits of partners can, however, make their intentions for commitments more realistic. Those traits would help them reconcile their problems easier and thus maintain a relatively healthy marital relationship. The opposite is also true: Without these compatibility factors, the chance of marriage success is slim. It does not matter how much they promise or even pretend to be making a compromise, they would not succeed without some inherent sense of commitment.

Tolerance and Patience

Partners' ability to distinguish and tolerate their moderate differences, rather than turning them into irreconcilable issues, is the backbone of all marriages. Without tolerance and patience, we break under the first wave of marital difficulties and decide to escape the stressful situation instead of trying to find sensible solutions. Yet, most of us do not realize the high level of patience and tolerance required, nowadays, not as a personal sacrifice but a harsh new reality in relationships. Most marital problems erupt nowadays from Ego conflicts and struggles about who is right and who is stubborn. There are often no major problems and, in fact, partners may even like each other in spite of their raw personalities and ongoing frictions. Under these circumstances, false pride and stubbornness often goad partners to declare war and go for separation. Usually, tolerance and patience (to override false pride and stubbornness) would help partners cool down initially and then come to some personal understanding of mutual problems eventually.

Managing Anger

Anger is a common, natural reaction. However, what we do with it, and how much we are able to control it, is important.

The ability to deal with anger is partly genetic and partly learnable. As a factor of compatibility, we should look for our partner's, as well as our own, ability to deal with anger. Most often anger erupts when either or both partners are highly opinionated, egotistical, and must have the final say in everything all the time. Unless one partner does not mind being dominated by his/her partner, eventually resistance and frictions lead to alienation and separation.

Ability to Forgive

Another factor of compatibility is partners' genuine capacity to forgive instead of being spiteful and reactionary. Naturally, when one partner makes a mistake, spite and retaliation would not solve the problem. If the mistake is too harsh and hurtful to one partner and cannot really be forgiven even after a period of cool down, then perhaps not much is left to do but to seek separation. However, if the mistake is not really an intentional or extreme disappointment for the victimized partner, s/he should have the ability to forgive if they are both willing and able to learn something from this experience. Sometimes, the victimized partner continues to live with his/her partner with the intention or thoughts of retaliation, which would only increase alienation and suffering for both partners. Therefore, partners should measure their own and their partner's ability to forgive and learn from their mistakes. These abilities are not difficult to observe and assess during the initial courtship.

Compassion

The level of compassion is indirectly helpful in keeping partners compatible. It is an important personality attribute that keeps our Ego under control. In fact, the ability to forgive, control anger, and exercise tolerance are all parts of one's compassion and outlook on life in general. A sign of snobbery reflects low compassion whereas some degree of humility in conjunction with subtle confidence can be a sign of compassion and tolerance. We can assess this factor as well.

The four personality attributes, i) tolerance, ii) forgiveness, iii) dealing with anger, and iv) compassion comprise the third set of compatibility factors that make partners' commitments to each other sensible and possible. If one or both partners are weak in many of these areas, the problems of alienation and frictions are inevitable. However, two additional points should be noted here as well.

First, partners should make their business to grasp the meaning, and think, of commitment as an essential part of marriage. We cannot think or make promises of commitment without really knowing what it means, how it can be achieved, and what its *real* objective is. Once this basic requirement is understood, we should actively look for 'sensible commitment factors' that were discussed above and measure them in ourselves and our partners.

Second, we must make it our business, at the outset, to share our expectations from marriage frankly and seriously with our partner and insist that s/he does the same. It is extremely important for partners to know about each other's major expectations from marriage, as well as their common objectives, personal goals, and what they are willing to do, or not do, for keeping their relationship intact.

Expressing their expectations honestly helps partners cross the bridge between *love* and *understanding*, while there is a bridge to make this crossover possible. The difference between love and understanding is usually unknown to partners, and remains unresolved before marriage. Partners believe they understand each other already and that nothing would change their wonderful impressions about marriage afterwards. They neglect to think practical because of their misperceptions of marriage. They assume their partner understands their expectations even better later and more automatically just because they are married. They think that living as a couple would in-crease the level of mutual understanding and sensitivity, and thus discussing and resolving expectations would be easy and a routine process. They might even imagine that their under-standings of each other's needs and expectations would be quite natural, and thus unnecessary to discuss in advance. This wishful thinking is a normal and natural feeling, but in reality it almost never happens. In fact, it seems that partners' level of understanding and responding to each other's expectations di-minishes fast after marriage. The list of compatibility factors (Table 3.1) is developed from the above discussions to use for assessing our partners and the prospects of our marriages.

Table 3.1: Compatibility Measure Relationships Success Factors
1. Compatibility to increase life enjoyments
• Physical attraction
• Communication and negotiation abilities
• Activities and thoughts to share
2. Compatibility for support and cooperation
• Teamwork
• Support to pursue personal goals
• Functional and psychological support
• Joint problem solving capabilities
3. Compatibility for a sensible commitment
• Tolerance
• Forgiveness
• Dealing with anger
• Compassion
• Awareness of commitment
• Expressing personal expectations

Personality Compatibility

Aside from the big list of compatibility measures (relationship success factors), partners' peculiar personality attributes and eccentricities can help or hinder their relationship. In particular, the three personality aspects of individuals (i.e., Ego, Model, and Self) play major roles in the presentation of a person's personality and his/her ability to get along with others. In a nutshell, Ego accounts for a person's strive for security and fulfilling his/her aspirations; Model mostly reflects his charisma and adaptation ability; and Self is the level of love and spirituality he can access in the depth of his being.

Refined studies are necessary to establish how partners' three personality aspects may interact for optimizing their compatibility. Obviously, if both partners have strong Self orientation, they have the highest chance of compatibility and relating. Outside this least likely scenario, couples with moderate Ego and Model dominations could possibly relate within a certain relationship model too. Thus, the idea is to explore the possibility of measuring the compatibility of less perfect personalities within various types of relationship models. (Relationship models will be designed more explicitly in the near future. However, for a general review of these models, you can study this author's books, *Relationship Needs, Framework, and Models*, or *The Nature of Love and Relationships*.)

Ego and Model affect relationships extensively these days. Ego reflects mostly a demanding personality and Model is too needy. With a reasonable level of Model and Ego, people can usually get along just fine. Only the excessive tendency in either or both Model and Ego makes a relationship intolerable. The other challenge is to determine which personality dominations of partners can possibly match, if at all. Is there any chance for people with relatively higher domineering Ego or Model to ever find a suitable relationship? We may not be able to find a definite answer before doing some detailed research. To be on the safe side, people must stay away from personalities with excessive Ego and Model dominations. These conditions make the chances of teamwork remote and most likely never lead to a healthy and productive relationship environment.

Nevertheless, partners must not only measure their Ego and Model intensity, but also determine partners' tolerance level required in relationships when Model and Ego are rather high. Presently, an accurate measurement of these personality aspects in a person is difficult, however. This is due to not only the lack of a reliable method, but also because people fake their personalities readily during the initial stages of their relationships. Gauging people's personalities is hard when they misrepresent themselves intentionally or inadvertently.

Often, our personality characteristics are not apparent or known even to us. Yet, they reside deep in our unconscious awaiting an opportunity to surface with a bang. For example, it is possible that a partner's extreme sense of anger and aggression have been repressed within him/her for many years, perhaps due to domineering and abusive parents. At some stage of life, these feelings may finally erupt in either an explosive or a gradual manner to reach an unbearable extreme. All the childhood traumas erupt in a destructive form, and most likely stay with the person for the rest of his/her life if something is not done about them. Nonetheless, most passive/aggressive people know how to fake their personalities in order to confuse or attract others.

Although not everybody can measure the intensity of his/her or another person's personality aspects with a good degree of accuracy, s/he can still determine reasonably how s/he stands on each aspect. Especially, if they are clever, they can do some quick tests to measure the intensity of another person's Ego or Model. They could even ask the opinion of an impartial third person. The mental guard that prospective marriage partners have toward each other is somewhat turned off or ineffective when they are with other people. Therefore, an outsider can notice hints of personality aspects that two partners would not reveal to, or detect about, each other.

A more difficult problem arises when we naively force ourselves into a doomed relationship. For example, we may have a domineering Ego or Model, but do not know, care, or do anything about it. We hide our flaws long enough until we win the love of someone we like to marry and then release our real personality. In this case, we hurt ourselves as much as our partners by getting into a potentially doomed marriage. We may or may not ever find the motivation and opportunity to overcome our personality deficiencies. Yet, marrying somebody while we have high Ego and Model tendencies would only lead to long-term suffering mostly by ourselves. Unless we learn to become a more rational and perhaps humbler person, not getting into serious relationships is the best choice for everybody, especially considering the potential damage on innocent children who end up facing their parents' animosity and fights. Yet, this is such a high expectation to place on selfish people with huge Egos.

Is Compatibility Only a Wishful Thinking?

We may think that we can assess our partner casually based on things s/he does or says. Seldom do we make direct and designed efforts to measure the particular aspects of compatibility, such as a person's ability to solve problems or honour his/her commitments. This is partly because we do not know how, and partly because it is not part of our social norms yet, although we judge people hastily anyway. While indirect and casual assessment has some value, it is not useful like a direct and designed test that we can actively develop and implement. Indirect assessments are based on our perfunctory judgments (and possibly even hasty emotional justifications) of our partner's calculated actions and behaviours. S/he can lie or use

Model to portray a different personality than s/he deeply is. In direct testing, however, we may create situations and ask questions that disable Model to play a prominent role, thus giving our partner's deeper personality attributes a chance to emerge.

A hurdle for gauging partners' compatibility lies in the fact that they mostly meet by accident, without any prior planning to look for certain qualities or even knowing what compatibility means for them. In fact, if we adhere to our rigid definition of compatibility factors, it seems that only personal perfection can guarantee compatibility. That is, only individuals with no or minimal psychological shortfalls, who are well aware of their needs and respect their partners' needs, can be compatible. The rest of us, who have some kind of psychological deficiency, are goaded by our Egos, and do not know what our partners or we need in terms of life enjoyment and support, have no chance of finding compatibility with anybody. We have no chance of having a comfortable life, because we can never be compatible with anybody, not even if our partner were a perfect human being. We personally and single-handedly ruin everything because of our egoism and insecurities. In the final analysis, it seems as if our own shortfalls make every one of us incompatible with the rest of the world.

Nevertheless, seeking compatibility is a major challenge, because we are too idealistic with our high expectations. While we keep looking for an ideal partner without knowing how to measure compatibility, no one can satisfy our needs, and at the end, it is mainly our own shortfalls that make us incompatible with everybody else, anyway. These facts suggest that most of us are doomed to suffer of incompatibility syndrome throughout our lives, mostly by our own faults. Not even professional help is available out there to measure partners' compatibility and give them at least a heads-up about looming headaches. The prevalent tests in the market nowadays, which claim to pinpoint partners' compatibility, are ineffective and flawed in terms of their designs.

How can we accept such a harsh truth and admit our flaws? Someday, we may be able to find better ways of searching and matching people through well-crafted mechanisms rather than depending on accidents to bring couples together. Of course, we can depend on computer matchmaking only when (sometime in the future) we have done sufficient research and understand which personal shortfalls of couples are possibly sharable between them, if at all possible. We must learn how couples may be mutually tolerant of each other. We need this tool, so that we can bring even less perfect people together harmoniously while pointing out their incompatibilities, which they must remain vigilant about. A more challenging task, of course, is to find out how couples with clear incompatibilities can be helped, mainly psychologically, for a reasonably acceptable joint life with minimal frictions and sufferings.

More important than compatibility is learning patience and admitting that even relatively good relationships are hard to build with our type of mentality and considering human nature in general. We must also educate couples about marriage requirements, partners' compatibly factors, and the guidelines for relating. Surely, the objective is not to help only fully compatible people marry. Rather, the objective is to empower most couples who feel attracted toward each other build a good relationship for themselves through education, self-awareness, and compatibility tests.

Compatibility testing is useful mostly before marriage in hopes of predicting the likely outcome of a proposed relationship. This can help couples to choose the right partner and relationship model for them. But then, once the decision is made, couples should try hard to make their relationship work in the best ways possible instead of arguing and blaming each other.

Overall, it is wise to hesitate and postpone the marriage until partners have had a chance to overcome all their doubts about compatibility factors, overall risks, and circumstances of their union, especially about the personality of both partners. If, at the end of their long evaluation, they still have doubts about some aspects of their compatibility and the prospects of their marriage, then most likely something is missing. That kind of union would fail.

On the other hand, couples must study the sources of their doubts. Many factors, including our natural (or obsessive) search for compatibility, our high expectations from companionships, and the necessity for partners' consensus on personal and joint objectives, goad us not to accept anything less than perfection. Unfortunately, this ideal is infeasible and not recommended here either. A complete match and compatibility is unrealistic. The idea is only to learn about the *practical* forms of compatibility for various relationship models and then evaluate our unique situation against it to gauge the level of discrepancy and potential for future headaches. If there is not enough compatibility or agreement on essential factors for the success of a relationship, then it is wise to stop. In particular, it is important to measure partners' compatibility factors for a specific 'relationship model' that best fits their mentalities and personal needs, especially for independence.

The bottom line is that, we must spend enough time to study certain essential traits and attributes of our prospective partner patiently, instead of deciding hastily, either positively or negatively. In particular, we should learn about those imperfections that we must cope with. Despite all the love we feel for a person, we should know realistically how we might tolerate those irritants and small nuisances, which are evident already, for many years to come without losing our sanity. Even small irritants and problems most likely lead to 'divorce.' Therefore, time for a right decision is now, while we also appreciate that no couple can be fully compatible!

A common mistake, which becomes evident only after marriage, is that one or both partners assume and perceive they are getting into a perfect, or at least a normal, marriage.

After marriage, they seek, and insist on, the *perfection* they had imagined for a 'normal' relationship, and instead only get more disappointments, distress, fights, retaliations, and alienation. Partners must realize at the outset that most likely they are not a perfect match, but more importantly why and in what respects, and how they can make their marriage work despite the known, and potentially a lot more, imperfections. A *normal* relationship is far from perfection and, in fact, it is full of inconveniences and quarrels. We also should be careful with our personal definition of perfection. We usually expect others to be perfect in the way we define perfection for our convenience and according to our personal values in life. In addition to this naïve demand, we allow ourselves to be and behave anyway we like—supposedly perfect—again as it suits us. We look at the world and people for our convenience, interests, and out of pure selfishness.

CHAPTER FOUR
Marriage Decision

IN the author's opinion, marriage is the second most critical decision nowadays in a normal life circumstance— next to the matter of separation and divorce after a long co-habitation. The process of deciding 'to marry or not to marry' a specific person is quite delicate and difficult. This is because we are not aware even of our own psychological needs and defects, and have no knowledge of our prospective partner's deep emotions and needs either. We undermine the complexities of marital life, due to our inexperience and naivety during the courting stage. Thus, we are not prepared for the demands and commitments that marriage places upon us. We do not know anything about relationships' specific needs. We do not know how to assess our common objectives, personal needs and expectations, and the unique features of our personalities. We do not know how to prepare ourselves for new challenges and changes in our lives.

In all, marriage demands real and often difficult changes, contrary to our imagination of a wonderful world that it would be. We should realize that some changes are necessary and useful, but perhaps not the ones that our spouse would like to impose upon us. We must test our sense, ability, and willingness to change, since after marriage 'independence' is no longer a strong feature of our new identity as a spouse. We must prepare ourselves by acknowledging and understanding the need for some personal adjustments, and also learn how to do them and why. We must change our attitudes and expectations and learn to use our Model (the personality aspect for coping) more than what we have learned or believe in. We should learn quickly to defeat the evil of domination and possessiveness in ourselves, or else expect a life of misery, contradictions, and quarrels.

Unfortunately, most people make their marriage decision spontaneously instead of systematically with proper knowledge of relationship needs and demands. Couples might be together unmarried for years, while making all kinds of judgments and assessments about each other and a marriage, too. Yet, the final decision to get married usually happens within days, if not hours or minutes, with one partner proposing and the other accepting, and viola we have a *shoddy* commitment and a *risky* marriage. What happens at this moment for such a crucial decision is usually unclear to the partners making and accepting the proposal, but it is mostly a matter of sentimentality and a hasty, spontaneous response to a surge of sudden personal urges. They simply cannot live without each other! Fine, but why get married, if not the issues discussed in this book are not quite clear to them? Nonetheless, this spontaneity and approach for marriage decision is risky and problematic in relationships nowadays. Partners imagine that they have already thought through their marriage scenario long enough, maybe even for years, but most likely they have not yet analysed the right factors realistically.

Marriage decision should always follow an educational process and never be a spontaneous act (like an outburst of emotions). The process should entail a plan of analyses and negotiations between partners until all the details of their future relationship are examined and worked out. This process might take a week, a month, or more to complete, at which point partners must be fully comfortable with all the details of their well-planned future relationship, including a partnership agreement that addresses all the issues raised in this book. At the end of this process, the marriage decision becomes obvious one way or another automatically without the need of one partner proposing it spontaneously and the other accepting or rejecting it equally unprepared. Instead of making a proposal, partners should only decide whether it is time to explore the possibility of marrying. If yes, then let the process begin, which includes the matter of learning about *'divorce' at the time of marriage* requirement. Only the details of a relationship must determine the outcome of the decision, only after partners have spent ample time to sort out all the angles totally. The present mode of marriage decision is outdated and inappropriate for such an extremely critical business. Marriage decision must be viewed and handled similar to signing a major treaty, which requires plenty of negotiating and planning. We should also learn about potential marriage agonies on top of the hassles of divorce, which a highly likely outcome of most marriages nowadays.

Assessing Marriage Agonies

We wish we had had foresight and wisdom about marital agonies always too late, only when marriage conundrums is overwhelming us and we are cursing the person who invented the idea of marriage. We recall the story of Adam and Eve's first meeting and remind ourselves of the tyranny of relationships. Yet, almost all of us ignore assessing both our marriages and divorces logically and deeply enough.

In fact, we should learn to view marriage and divorce decisions in a rather reverse order. That is, we should think and discuss divorce (consequences) at the time of marriage, and think and discuss marriage (intentions) when contemplating divorce. We should use this proactive principle in evaluating our marriage and divorce decisions. The purpose and benefits of this idea will be elaborated shortly. First, however, let us imagine our partners' most likely reaction to this cynical proposal and review the practicality of thinking about, and discussing, divorce at the time of marriage.

Naturally, it sounds depressing and dubious to think and discuss divorce when we are planning our wedding and all its related joyful events. We are hesitant to contemplate or raise this insensitive issue, because we do not wish to spoil all the romantic mood. We do not dare to disturb even our own feelings of love and joy, let alone suggesting a discussion of such pessimistic nature to our prospective partner. It is unromantic, for sure, and our partners would react and resist listening to our seemingly negative and calculating thoughts, and then asking him/her to share his/her views too! Yet, those reactions and resistance are all part of the evaluation process too. We would be labelled uncompassionate and paranoiac. However, allowing these thoughts stop us from doing a proper evaluation would be our first mistake in marital life. If our views agitate our partners, the situation would present a good opportunity to predict (and measure) his/her way of reacting during tough times and use this information for our final decision. It is wise to arouse, now, those hidden emotions that would definitely erupt later in marriage. In fact, it is necessary to initiate the process of unravelling partners' thoughts regarding sensitive matters and examining their ability to negotiate and compromise. All these issues would come out for discussion and dispute sooner or later, so why not sooner? The romantic mood we are trying so hard not to spoil subsides shortly after marriage anyway. You can bet all your physical and mental assets on that!

Most of us hide foolishly behind our emotions and resist the truth we know or hear about marital life. However, avoiding the truth would neither help us now with our decision about this serious commitment, nor change its outcome once the relationship realities and emotions erupt like a volcanic mess. Therefore, we are definitely better off to test the waters now. For example, if we think that it is necessary to have a prenuptial agreement, we should not hesitate to discuss it with our partner on the ground that it may spoil the mood. Of course, if we are **absolutely** sure that such an agreement is not practical or necessary, talking about it as a hypothetical condition might not help too much, though it would not hurt either. Nevertheless, we should be very careful with our interpretation of 'practical and necessary' and do not let our timidity force us choose an optimistic position about the future of our marriage. On the contrary, always work from the worst-case scenario position.

But what do we mean by discussing divorce at the time of marriage? The purpose of thinking and discussing divorce in advance is to contemplate the scenario in which divorce becomes inevitable. After all, this is a very likely scenario in modern societies. Thus, as a starting point, we should read books about divorce and learn about the headaches of irreconcilable marriages, where couples face unbearable circumstances. We should learn about the hassles and pains of divorce, or being trapped in an unpleasant or unproductive relationship. Many marriages end up in this position, because partners do not have the courage or resources to pursue other options or start all over with a new relationship subsequent to a divorce. Therefore, by contemplating divorce, we like to do two things:

First, we study the most common impact of divorce on individuals emotionally, psychologically, physically, and financially in general. Many books and articles about divorce and its effects on individuals and their children are available. This background would help a lot. The amount of time we invest on this education is the most justifiable and profitable project of our life. The more time we spend on understanding the hassles of a bad marriage and divorce, the more time and money we save in life, even compared to the most profitable business venture we have ever done.

Second, we try to predict the potential causes and consequences of divorce according to our particular situation and personality. We can imagine future events under most probable scenarios and then project our position and reactions. Certainly, our position and feelings at the time of divorce varies according to many factors, particularly the years of being married and our age. Anticipating our feelings in such a position, in a distant future, is difficult, but not impossible. After getting a basic impression of the devastating effects of divorce, try to multiply it ten folds to possibly gain a more realistic sense.

For example, we can learn that the sense of loss and desperation after divorce are many folds more severe than the feelings of losing a mere companion, which we are most likely familiar with already. In spite of equal love in 'marriage' and 'companionships,' the pain of unfulfilled commitments and expectations after divorce are many folds more intense compared with separation in a simple companionship. We can learn that the sense of loneliness and failure after a marriage breakdown would be much harsher and more suffocating than the loneliness we feel during bachelorhood when we are young and have not gone through many years of marital life dependency and conveniences. The feelings of loneliness intensify exponentially according to our age too. If we find loneliness intolerable now that we are young and full of urges for independence, we might be able to imagine the shock and the sour feeling of separation after a long marital experience. During marriage, we gradually lose our sense of independence and become fully conditioned to a new way of life as years go by. We become softer and more vulnerable to the feeling and state of loneliness after many years of joint life. In a sense, it would be preferable to stay unmarried and hold on to our sense of self-reliance than marrying, becoming vulnerable, and then being left alone and confused. Reading some books on 'how to cope with divorce' would show the immense level of troubles and confusion that a divorce experience causes. The feeling of loneliness is only one of many hardships and consequences of divorce. We feel cheated and deprived out of a fruitful life. We feel like a loser. We feel unappreciated, misunderstood, abused, and so much more. Most of us would, eventually, after a few months or years, overcome the primary feelings of loss and loneliness as we gain our sense of independence partially. However, there would always be some deep scars that we would carry for the rest of our lives.

The task of evaluating divorce scenarios is not easy, but most importantly it is not intended to cause apprehension and paranoia about marriage. We only want to make our decision of marriage as educated as possible. And the fact is that no knowledge is more relevant about marriage than the information about divorce. Next to a review of hypothetical divorce facts and scenarios, an assessment of partners' positions and characters at the present time is also useful. This assessment includes a complete review of partners' assets and liabilities brought into this partnership, financially, emotionally, psychologically, and physically. This is the time to measure partners' capacity, mostly in terms of inherent compassion and intelligence, to share a joint life and relate.

Thinking divorce at the time of marriage is meant to be an educational process to prepare both partners for a productive relationship according to a viable relationship model, or stop them from making a big mistake (i.e., marriage) that they would be sorry about. No amount of time spent on this educational process—until partners are absolutely sure one way or other—is ever a waste. They should prepare a proper agreement in writing to demonstrate their initial efforts to make the right decision, but also remember all these conversations and promises. Many of these issues and agreements would help in preparing and signing a marriage contract. Two people can live together for as long as it is necessary to figure out all these details and study each other's temperament, patience, etc. Then, if they wish, they can write the agreement and make their cohabitation official, if they really think marriage has some tangible benefits.

All these discussions of 'thinking divorce at the time of marriage' would become also handy for choosing a proper relationship model. Partners must understand the implications of relating within that type of environment (a particular relationship model) and learn about the factors that are essential for maintaining a relationship with minimal frictions. Partners' discussions also prepare them for negotiating the topics that become most contentious when the possibility of divorce comes to fore in the future. At that point (when divorce seems inevitable), remembering their initial conversations and contract would prove most useful. It would be the best time to 'think of marriage at the time of divorce.' Divorce is discussed in detail in Part II. The newlyweds or those who are considering marriage are particularly encouraged to read all the chapters in Part II very carefully.

Developing a Partnership Agreement

We all live with a strong sense of romanticism and hope. Yet, marriage should be viewed as a business partnership more than anything else. The real life and marriage environment cannot be any further different from the image that nowadays the naïve public builds from love stories and movies. All the evidence from family relationships and divorce statistics indicate that, in modern societies, marital life turns into a business partnership anyway with partners fighting hard for their rights and equities. Therefore, with this eventuality in sight, we should start it as a business as well. Partners are quite adamant and ultra careful nowadays that everything, even their simplest household activities, is handled equally and fairly by both partners, let alone their financial issues. Marriage nowadays appears like a business partnership that has been put together hastily without partners knowing about the business they were getting into, their capitals and assets, and their shares of total equity in case the business were dissolved, etc. In the absence of a better system, judicial systems follow the rule of 50/50 asset distribution for almost all cases. Surely, this cannot be an equitable formula since income level and contributions of partners can never be exactly equal. Of course, all other purposes of marriage are also important and will be shortly discussed too. However, we should initiate our evaluation process with business factors, because, in the final analysis, money always becomes the main issue, especially when partners get to the divorce stage.

Partners' discussions of their financial affairs do not focus only on equity build-up and distribution. Financial matters include many sensitive issues that normally cause major nuisances and clashes in relationships. The matters of family budget, savings, investments, and financial controls play major roles in family affairs and create painful arguments and frictions, because they are not discussed and decided upon at the outset. Then, after marriage, a partner who is more domineering and demanding initiates subtle tactics, or perhaps even forceful manoeuvres, to take over all these affairs, with the other partner losing influence and voice in most matters. At best, all these contentious issues become the sources of arguments, conflicts, retaliations, and all kinds of nastiness that soon erupts in most relationships.

Personal independence in marriage is jeopardized due to not only emotional needs, but also loss of control on financial freedom and personal preferences. Arguments and disagreements start about who should be responsible for what, whether all income should go to one account, how, and who decides about the necessities of life versus savings, the kinds of investments, the manner and details of investments, etc. These matters require mutual understanding and good faith. More importantly, however, they require good skills in negotiating and assertiveness. Negotiating and assertiveness before marriage can mitigate a *reasonable portion* of the arguments and aggressiveness that normally ensue after marriage. Except that partners should remember to remain assertive, calm, objective, and willing to negotiate after marriage as well. One partner should not let emotions and subtle tactics of the other partner influence him/her to give up some of the rights s/he had established for him/herself before marriage. Loss of independence and financial controls usually happen gradually when one partner finds the opportunity to penetrate his/her partner's soft spots and take charge eventually. When the controlled partner realizes these manoeuvres, s/he can either cope and suffer, or get into horrendous waves of fights and struggles, and then, most likely, go for separation.

Prospective marriage partners should agree on an equitable scheme for financial contributions and distribution of income and wealth, but also securing partners' financial independence. Combining their income, investments, bank accounts, etc. is not the right approach for the new era. The main features of this agreement should be put in writing and signed by both partners. Even better, some issues may be prepared and witnessed legally to protect partners against future claims and demands. The scheme should definitely be fair, flexible and friendly and treated as a financial plan for mutual understanding. On occasions when one partner does not work or does not have income due to family or other reasons, the other partner should make a higher financial contribution toward the family expenses. However, partners should have their own savings and investments, while they could have joint savings and investments too, if they both desire, but not as a mandatory requirement dictated by one partner. The financial schemes are not supposed to reflect tight controls and measures for everything. The idea is to retain personal controls and independence over one's financial affairs even after marriage. Partners would be generous toward each other without having to account to their partners on what they do with their monies beyond what is agreed to for joint family expenses and capital purchases like a home, car, etc.

In this agreement, partners should also discuss and document each partner's share of work and activities around the house, especially when children are born. These tentative arrangements are, of course, adjustable in the future by negotiation and goodwill. All we need to establish before marriage is a sense of joint responsibility, comradeship, financial structure, flexibility, and good intentions. Above all, this process would establish a mutual understanding of partners' needs (now and in the future), their negotiating skills, and lay out the foundation for a cooperative atmosphere that should prevail in a healthy marriage. Hopefully!

When a partner dishonours his/her initial agreement on the ground that s/he was fooled into signing it, the usual problems begin. It is a good practice to have a third party grasp, explain, and witness the intentions of the agreement, so that the excuse of not understanding or being coerced into it cannot stand. Obviously, without some level of faith and mutual trust between partners, they can write a ten-thousand-page agreement and still see it violated after the marriage. In all, hoping that partners stay rational, fair, and patient is naive and a good reason to doubt the value of the logical approaches discussed in this chapter. Yet, for the same reasons, we must be careful and take all these precautionary measures before marriage. Meanwhile, we can hope that someday soon we all need to be a bit more logical and practical. Soon, we should have standard marriage contracts available to the public, so that they can only fill out some selected clauses and have it signed. There would not be a need for partners to start writing all the details down themselves, but only follow the format and guidelines offered in these standard contracts. The process would feel more natural and necessary as well, when standard contract forms are used.

The purpose of a 'marriage evaluation process' prior to the wedding is to bring to surface any areas of major personality differences and potentials for future clashes. This process is also useful for educating the young partners about the potential conundrums in marriage and getting themselves ready for facing them rationally. It also helps them learn about these basic (but essential) requirements of marriage, i.e., financial and teamwork aspects of marriage. All the predictable, contentious issues in a marriage that couples are often ignorant about should be highlighted in standard contracts so that partners get a chance to learn about them and spend time pondering them. Moreover, if a partner changes his/her mind about a written commitment or agreement, we still know that we had done our homework in communicating our fair expectations at the outset. If a marital relationship suffers, it would be because of the new ideas and expectations that a partner suddenly tries to introduce and impose upon his/her partner. Normally, partners should not agree with each other's new ideas and demands, unless they seem reasonable, in which case their initial agreement should be modified properly and formally. However, again, partners must make sure they are not manipulated, which is sometimes hard to know.

A major marital problem develops when one partner notices a sudden change of position in the other partner. Especially, when partners do not talk about family budget, work, income, and other arrangements before marriage, the partner who has withheld his/her demands suddenly finds the courage and urge to discuss his/her emotions and needs. This would not only come across as a change of personality, but also a sign of rebellion to the other partner. If partners have a chance to express their demands (which could in fact reflect their legitimate needs) at the time of creating their marriage agreements, the perception of 'personality change' and new demands would less likely erupt and cause a big shock and friction between partners later.

Finding the courage to pursue the thoughts and steps of preparing an agreement with our partner is a major task nowadays. Yet, this would become a natural and common practice in the near future, simply because it would reduce the problems that often emerge after marriage drastically, or prevent those potentially doomed and risky marriages. A little bit of time and controversy at the beginning, before marriage, would not only save tons of time and hassle at the time of separation, but also strengthen the marriage. A judicial system should find ways to recognize and force a prenuptial agreement, but also facilitate the process of preparation and legal documentation of these agreements. All the time and efforts spent on negotiating and preparing an agreement is fully justified. It saves a lot of time, money, and agony later. Especially, the extra work before marriage, when we are younger, is more tolerable than doing ten times more work and bearing all the extra pain of divorce when we are older and have less energy and patience. Partners should really take their time now that they are supposedly in love, energetic, calm and collected, instead of pulling their own and each other's hairs during the stressful period of divorce as two ferocious enemies.

The idea of viewing marriage as a business partnership would appear ridiculous, insensitive, and impractical to us. When we feel love toward someone, our eyes, ears, and brains go on vacation and refuse to consider the simplest suggestions or words of wisdom, let alone bothering with business transactions that hinder the prospect of winning someone's love. Those romantic feelings of love that we read in poetry books are true and apply to all of us to some degree. They fool all of us. When we believe we love somebody, we can give everything we have and sacrifice even ourselves just for having his/her love or even the mere honour of his/her company. Nothing else matters to us at that moment except being part of his/her life now, forget what may happen in a few years. When we are in love, we undermine all the essential factors for a workable relationship and assume everything would work out nicely at the end. We naively believe that love would solve all the problems, even if 'love' is one-sided. However, in reality, the opposite is true: Peculiar relationship problems and widespread personal idiosyncrasies kill even mutual love very quickly. All those love stories in books and movies, as well as our own feelings of infatuation, are incredibly misleading and untrue.

Unfortunately (or fortunately), there is no remedy for love and its traps. As long as we hear and read about marriage and divorce facts, the victory of logic over emotions or vice versa would be a matter of personal character. The option of living with our lover before marriage is helpful in restraining the overwhelming infatuation, so that logic may find a chance for evaluating the hidden facts. However, even cohabiting may not solve the problems for many reasons. Partners may become dependent and addicted to each other's love and cohabitation conveniences before they get a chance to express their needs and negotiate a fair deal that would help their relationship in the long run. More importantly, however, people's real character often emerges only after marriage. People change a lot too, so unexpectedly, especially when some new adventures or financial incentives lure them.

Aside from love entrapment—even when we believe we are immune to the blinding effects of love, and when we believe we are a logical person—we can still get trapped in a relationship for some other irrational thoughts or beliefs. In particular, we usually think, "Why should I go through the hassle of evaluating divorce scenarios and viewing marriage as a business *when I know and trust my partner* already?"

Knowing Our Partner

Many of this author's writings emphasize on the task of 'knowing ourselves' to enrich our lives and avoid life's traps. Our ability to understand our needs and ourselves helps our relationships too. Yet, knowing 'who we are' is a challenging venture, even if we acknowledge a need for it. Those absorbed in their Egos, especially, believe they know who they are very well already. Realistically, however, it takes a lot of effort, perseverance, modesty, and motivation to learn 'who we are.'

We are supposedly a conscious judge of our actions, emotions, and thoughts, yet remain doubtful forever as to 'who we really are.' We cannot penetrate enough into our unconscious mind to find out the truth about our essence—the 'self,' which holds the secret of 'who we are.' We touch and feel certain traces of it from time to time when some novel dimensions of our existence unfold in front of our eyes unexpectedly, often through a profound thought or a deep sensation, perhaps love for another person.

We might discover certain things about ourselves and our 'self' gradually if we are patient and persistent. Often, our discovery is enlightening or shocking to us. Yet, knowing who we are is a difficult and lengthy process despite our supposedly analytical brains, objectivity, deep convictions and thoughts, and all the controls we believe to have over our behaviour, emotions, judgments, and attitudes. Therefore, finding who we really are remains only an abstract idea for most of us.

Now, if knowing 'who we are' is next to impossible in spite of our relative control over 'self,' just imagine how difficult it would be for any of us to know 'who they are.' How naive we should be to think that we know our partner completely. This is practically impossible because even our partner would not know 'who s/he is,' let alone an outsider who surely has no access even to her/his conscious or subconscious.

The situation gets even more complicated in close relationships. Not only we think we know who we are and who they are, but also **we assume they (our prospective partners) know 'who they are.'** We assume that the way our partner is presenting her/himself to us is based on his/her knowledge of who s/he is, or s/he is at least honest about his/her presentations of his/her character. In reality, however, our partner is not only unaware of who s/he is, but most likely confused about his/her identity like the rest of us. We assume that all of his/her reactions and judgments are well studied and coordinated according to some logical and valid knowledge of who s/he is, when in reality s/he is drawing on any of his/her three aspects of personality to deal with us at any time often with little conscious or conscience.

There are still other erroneous assumptions on our part. Not only we think we know who we are and who they are, and not only we assume that they know who they are and they remain faithful to who they are in dealing with us, **we also assume they know 'who we are.'** How many times have we heard ourselves complain and feel disappointed when we thought that our partner did not know us (after all this time)? And still we continue with our poor logic to assume that s/he should have known us and our expectations, because we have tried to explain everything to them so many times (god knows through which aspect of our personality). The simple fact is that even if our partner was smart and motivated enough to attempt to know 'who we are,' s/he would not be able to really find out who we are for the same reason we would never know who they are. It is too naive to expect people understand us. Others understand us according to their perceptions, which is always a limited point of view. This matter gets even more complicated when all of us try to display a fake personality of ourselves in order to fit in or get accepted. We try to hide our naiveté and instead become too haughty to assert ourselves and prove our identity.

The process of knowing 'who we are' and 'who they are' extends a few more levels. For example, we can ponder the case in which we assume our partner believes that we know 'who we are,' etc. Or, we may think that what we do not know about our partner's family background, genes, and rearing experiences do not affect the outcome of a relationship. However, in most situations they do. Parents and close relatives sometimes interfere and influence our married lives directly and indirectly too.

One main hurdle for knowing ourselves and our partners is that we resort to different aspects of our personality to communicate with, and manipulate, one another. Very seldom we use our 'self' aspect of personality in our encounters to remain sincere. If we did, we would have a much better chance to understand and know one another. Instead, we use our Ego and Model more often to hide our intentions and secrets, and to satisfy our egoistic needs. Using different aspects of our personality does not only prevent us from knowing who we are and who they are. It also contaminates the content and meaning of relationships. We pretend to be a nice person to attract someone we think we love or want to make love to. We hide our tremendous egoism and selfish desires until the initial love fever subsides. We learn about humans' vulnerability and use this knowledge to manipulate one another as much as we can. For example, we manipulate our partner with our fake compliments just to boost his/her Ego. The strange thing about human nature is that we welcome these compliments even when we know they are insincere.

In many instances, we block the channels of information subconsciously and inadvertently. For example, when we are in love, we keep justifying our partners' intentions. Our 'love need' is simply too strong to give logic and common sense a chance. We just do not want to lose our companion even if we have to deceive ourselves by closing our minds to the obvious signs of egoism and bad character that radiates readily from our prospective partner. We continue to give a benefit of a doubt to our partner, but at the same time build a barrel of doubts about who we and our partners are. These doubts do not get resolved as long as we keep justifying our own or our partners' actions and intentions. This accumulation of doubts about our partners and ourselves hurt our relationships and psyches. We fight with our rising inner conflicts while we cannot think straight or accept the risk of losing the person we love.

Without getting into more details for our narrow purpose in this book, it suffices to remember that partners' naïve assumptions about knowing each other is hardly correct, even if they have been in love and a long-term relationship. Those naïve assumptions become direct causes for stress and major disappointments. It is even more amazing that we intentionally ignore even the obvious signs of personality issues and crooked motives of a person when we seemingly fall in love with him/her or feel lonely.

PART II

Divorce

CHAPTER FIVE
Divorce Decision

THE most difficult decision, under normal life circumstances, comes about when a marital relationship breaks down, especially if young children are involved. Not only the agony of separation and legal hassles, but also deep scars hurt partners and their children for many years. Most divorced individuals agree with this assertion. On the other hand, married couples gauge their options regularly, while their hardships due to alienation compete with the prospects of separation and divorce agonies. When partners' defects are extensive and obvious, the decision is easy. However, a separation decision often gets tough because most people have borderline psychological flaws—which still make them incompatible and wicked—and yet the decision becomes only a matter of partners' tolerance level.

Partners' imperfections, which often appear normal individually, clash in relationships severely, and thus the degree of their incompatibility and malice increases many folds very quickly. At the same time, partners are unable to set their tolerance level realistically, because they have no reliable view of the expected (acceptable) level of conflicts in relationships. Without enough self-control and wisdom, they let their Egos drive all their decisions, including the matter of a desired tolerance level for a typical marital relationship. In fact, many people are less willing or able nowadays to live with the inconveniences of marital life, mainly due to their drive for individuality and a misguided sense of self-importance. Therefore, with the first signs of problem, they look for a way out. Conversely, another group takes plenty of abuse, but are too weak to face the matter in a constructive way. The majority of us, however, fall between these two extremes. This group has adequate tolerance to accept some of the deficiencies of marital life, but also has enough pride to consider the option of separation if things REALLY do not work. This group usually has the most difficult time in making a decision, though, because not only it is never clear when to give up tolerating and depart, but also the repercussions of separation and divorce feel quite severe to these sensible people. As a result, we, the majority, must live with life and marriage hardships, but also struggle with our incessant doubts about the validity and viability of our marriage and the future of our confusing relationships. These doubts are quite overwhelming and often linger a lifetime.

This social dysfunction has obviously spread since we no longer know how to relate to one another in society. Especially in marriage, we walk into a trying trap, because most of us do not know enough about relationships' unique needs to make our marriage work, while getting out feels awkward and depressing too. It is a trap because the alternatives in most cases do not seem too lucrative, especially when our youth is wasted and there are many opposing factors to consider. **This is the kind of knowledge (point of reference) we must rely on for thinking divorce when contemplating marriage—** before getting trapped in a position where the alternatives to our miserable marriage appears even more depressing.

Separation is the most difficult life decision, because we often end up in a less favourable position than we like to be (or imagine initially). Opting for divorce carelessly or living with the agony of indecision about separation has its own stressful outcome. In either case, when we seek divorce prematurely or when we struggle to save our marriage futilely, we cause sufferings for ourselves and our children. Drawing on statistics, too many of us choose the divorce solution, because it seems easier and most appealing to our Ego too. In this state of mind, we consider divorce the only solution because we have tolerated enough already. Our false pride in particular has been damaged. And our sense of individualism, independence, and equality is threatened. However, perhaps we are not there yet and there is a chance for saving our relationship if we stop being antagonistic and hasty in arriving at such a negative conclusion. Therefore, this becomes **the point of reference (the reason) for thinking marriage when separation appears more viable and easier.** Thinking about marriage is the idea of creating an atmosphere for relaxing our mind to think through things more clearly.

We think of marriage in order to revive the mood of romanticism that started this relationship, which is needed now more than it had ever been. In addition, we think of marriage to pinpoint the issues that have contaminated a relationship that had seemed so logical at the time of marriage. What promises and factors had made the strength of this relationship? We want to explore what and how things have changed our relationship and us. We want to see whether we would come up with a different solution, if we could set our Ego aside a few days. We wish to evaluate the viability of forces that can keep us together to fulfil the *real* purposes of marriage instead of focusing on personal whims or fussing over irresolvable human issues. The question to ask is whether it is possible to remarry our partner after we have drifted apart inadvertently because of ignorance or egoism. Have we tried to communicate in a constructive manner to resolve our differences and to express our ideas in a logical manner? Have we become so alienated that separation seems to be the only solution? And for those of us who still have a chance to save their relationships, we should know what creates alienation. Moreover, we want to know how we have drawn the borderline between tolerance and divorce. We want to reset our expectations and list the criteria and rules that we find useful for relating with our partner within a new relationship model in order to salvage our marriage. We like to consider the possibility and conditions for remarrying our existing spouse if starting all over was a viable and sensible option.

Many divorces could have been avoided if partners had a little more tolerance and patience and had used their Self rather than allowing their Egos guide (deceive) them in such a crucial time. Our wild imaginations deceive us about a more caring and smarter partner waiting out there for us. We allow our false pride and stubbornness dictate the decision of separation and divorce, whereas compassion and forgiveness could have saved a lot of hassle and misery for both partners and their children. Conversely, we could have found at least some peace of mind and regained our independence if we had made a decision to separate from our spouse when the relationship did not seem to work out in spite of our efforts to reconcile our personality differences and marital deficiencies. The question partners should ask themselves is whether another relationship model exists for them to adopt for living together (maybe a bit more independently and passively if necessary) as an alternative to divorce.

The decision of separation and divorce is quite easy, and least consequential, when both partners *sincerely* and objectively believe that alternatives are definitely more promising and separation is to their advantage. A decision under this circumstance is easy if partners are in a sound mental condition to make an honest assessment of their needs. However, it is usually hard to be sincere in our beliefs (mostly about separation), because we do not know how to curb our Egos and fantasies even for a few days to gauge the situation realistically without bias and spite. The decision becomes difficult when our Egos take charge of the situation and ruin our objectivity even if we were a logical person. Ego diminishes our ability for tolerance and contemplation. Consequently, partners get engaged in endless pursuit of power struggles and petty shows of individualism (according to their own short-sighted definition of individualism and independence, of course). And when it is not egoism hindering the communication, partners do not know the mechanism of cooperating to resolve their problems, and thus resort to the option of separation.

In some extreme instances, one partner has special personal plans, extramarital affairs, or simply makes a unilateral decision about separation without paying any attention to the needs and desires of his/her partner. In these situations, separation would most likely be inevitable and the other partner is doomed to accept an imposed decision. It would be too late to convince the demanding partner to change his/her mind, and there is usually very little chance of reconciling their differences. One partner has already made the decision for both of them in such cases.

Pre and Post-Divorce Hardships

Our attempt to make a right decision about divorce causes a great deal of inner conflict, while we struggle and suffer on an alienation course incessantly. This topic is explained in the next chapter. When the decision is to separate, however, a new set of challenges overwhelm us. We must redefine ourselves as a fully independent person in our heads again and perform a barrage of duties on our own. Especially, the matter of raising kids almost single-handedly would prove to put a big burden on our psyches and other aspects of our lives. We like to find another companion, but the task would become increasingly frustrating and futile. The hassles of dealing with the legal process, child custody and sharing routines, financial pressures, and the agony of many quarrels on many issue with our ex-spouse could ruin our careers, mental state, and many years of our lives.

Indeed, post-divorce hardships are too horrendous and vast to include in this book in detail, but enough clues are made along the way. The emphasis in this book is on pre-divorce issues and hardships, because if we succeed to avoid a divorce we would be avoiding the much harsher hardships of post-divorce. The irony is that our misperceptions about marriage objectives and our opportunities after divorce often prevent us nowadays to analyse the state of our relationships honestly and realistically. We are lured into favouring a divorce decision prematurely. Thus, it is important to learn about the alienation process and debilitating 'separation thoughts' that most couples encounter in their relationships. If we learn about the hardships of all marriages and divorces, as well as our role to manage our relationships more effectively, we increase our chance for living a less hectic life and avoiding a big mistake.

Separation Path

Usually a long, rough path leads to separation. From the early days of honeymoon and love, we embark upon a journey in search of intimacy and a friendly relationship. However, like any journey, the road is full of hazards and turmoil. *Sneaky storms* erupt after we set sail so enthusiastically on this journey. Some obscure and adverse currents destroy our enthusiasm and redirect our focus toward a new, ambiguous destination. Our search for intimacy fails and we enter a new phase of relationship, which feels more like a journey of alienation. Every day we feel more estranged and drifting further apart from our partner until we hardly see or feel each other. Naturally, everybody abhors this looming destination and the depressing idea of 'separation.' This option had hardly crossed our minds when getting married; or maybe we recklessly dismissed the chance to study it. Somehow, however, we have arrived at this destination unexpectedly. We are shocked and confused, yet the reason for arriving at this point is clear: Estrangement happens when we lose sight of our initial destination (marriage purposes) and drift away mentally to a point where we cannot see our partner eye to eye; we cannot help each other stir the boat in the same direction. Therefore, when we arrive, it would be an odd destination where we had not sailed for, and we feel lonely, tired, and confused. We have just gotten there because we had drifted away from our original targets mostly out of ignorance, spite, and stubbornness.

The long, lonely journey of 'alienation' brings us deep disappointments, disagreements, hurts, turmoil, anger, and anxiety. Soon the time comes when our sweet dreams and love are gone and our relationship enters a new phase of constant doubts and evaluation. We assess our marriage, our partner, our expectations, and the prospect of the existing arrangement. A deep sense of doubtfulness and an urge to assess our options overwhelm our minds gradually, as we live in a haze with our pressing life responsibilities and struggles. We question the sensibility of our life and relationship and seek a solution. Our doubts about, and search for, a refuge intensify during marital conflicts or when we withdraw temporarily in a state of shock. Naturally, we are disappointed with the consequences of married life and build deep cynicism about the value and validity of marriage. The more we are disappointed and discouraged about our relationship and unfulfilled expectations, and the more we become doubtful of our sanity to live in this condition, the more we feel alienated toward our partner. Our initial attraction and trust are readily replaced by doubts, suspicions, and resentment.

If these thoughts and feelings sound familiar, you are most likely on an alienation course and now is time to do something about it fast.

The Turmoil

As partners are often unaware of their marital atmosphere and how poorly they relate to each other, they do not notice the alienation journey they are on until it is too late to return. They suddenly face a big turmoil. Perhaps when we are in the early stages of this journey, we could return to the main road, but not after we have travelled a long distance and fallen apart from our partner completely. We would simply not have enough stamina and motivation to travel back even if we could find the road to return. At some point and time, eventually the road to return is eroded by severe storms and upheavals. Some of us may be lucky in avoiding the alienation journey due to our personalities without even realizing it, but most of us are susceptible to embark upon this journey fast when our marital relationship start to deteriorate. If we are unaware of the hazards of this journey and unprepared to fight the traps of the alienation actively, we soon find ourselves in a no-return zone only able to move forward where the journey ends in turmoil, separation, or perhaps a lifelong of desolation at the very best.

Naturally, alienation is mainly the outcome of unmatched personalities unnoticed or ignored before marriage. When we discover our partner's shortfalls, and when we realize our naivety in trying to change him/her, we get discouraged and adopt an attitude of resistance or carelessness that leads to more conflicts and misunderstandings. We would rather withdraw than fight on issues that we finally accept as irresolvable and irreconcilable. Misunderstandings, poor communication skills, and other marital problems also contribute to alienation even if partners had been partially, or even totally, compatible. With our withdrawals, we fuel the process of alienation. In addition, initial respect and attraction fades away after a period of living together and learning about each other's idiosyncrasies. Thus, it gets almost impossible to reverse the course of alienation and separation. All that initial love and enthusiasm seem to vaporize and one or both partners wonder about the fast turn of events and loss of passion.

Reversing Our Focus

While it is wise to prevent mismatched marriages, our focus should reverse after marriage. That is, the burden of proof resides on partners' shoulders to demonstrate why their differences cannot be worked out if their psychological defects and Egos are not drastic and uncontrollable; and if the logic and some flares of love that existed at the time of marriage is still intact. Even unmatched partners may have a chance to reconcile their differences if they remain aware and resist the temptation of going deeply on an alienation journey.

A major problem is that we do not recognize the hidden traps in marriage and how they lead to alienation. Therefore, naively we leave the future of our marriage to chance and destiny, because we do not know how to play an active role in recognizing and avoiding alienation entrapments. Most cases of alienation relate to partners' inability to communicate properly, although they may be relatively compatible. In fact, even incompatible partners with mutual attraction and ability to communicate succeed better than matched couples who cannot learn to communicate. This is quite unfortunate because partners trap themselves on the alienation journey unnecessarily and wastefully. Another sizeable portion of separations is due to innocent miscommunications, which exhausts partners' patience and level of tolerance.

The process of alienation starts with small disappointments. However, these letdowns accumulate quickly when partners do not deal with them collectively and promptly. Staying conscious of the destructive power and outcome of alienation, partners can learn to fight the circumstances and personal urges that induce alienation. They can learn about those interactions and situations that cause misunderstanding, hurt feelings, and alienation. They should also understand the repercussions of their forbidding attitudes (including misperceptions, idiosyncrasies, and hasty judgments about their partner) as creators of alienation conditions and torments.

We can find all kinds of examples and typical situations that lead to alienation. For one thing, our (changing) image of our partner initiates the process of alienation. Our unfulfilled expectations of marital life and our perception of a perfect partner create major misunderstandings. We compare our partner's behaviour with our image of a perfect mate who can satisfy our needs. We merely focus on our own needs and convenience. When our partner cannot match that image, we become extremely disappointed and angry with him/her. Our inability to control our Ego, when we face such inconveniences, plays a major role in developing alienation.

The high demands and responsibilities of marriage also create alienation when the concepts of teamwork and sensible commitment are not understood and observed. Partners may still have the potential of increasing their life enjoyments together if other hurdles did not stop them. However, they cannot fulfil the main requirements of a successful marriage because they are not trained for married life properly. And of course, their inexperience regarding marital circumstances and its communication hurdles make them incapable of making the right judgments and decisions, at least in their first marriage. Usually our second and third marriages—if we ever dare to marry again—have a lesser chance of failure. Is this because we learn a few lessons about the intricacies of relationships and alienation entrapments from our first marriage? Or, we simply give up and decide to be more patient and tolerant, perhaps because we are getting older and feel more vulnerable? Or, because we have become wiser and realized that marriage can never be even slightly perfect, the way we like it to be? Or, because we are now more careful and knowledgeable about our selection of a companion? Perhaps a combination of all these factors. Yet, many of these lessons could be learned beforehand and practiced in the first marriage as well, if we just invest some time and patience.

The Effect of Global Mentality

We usually use a collection of simple examples to arrive at general and global interpretations. This time, we can do the opposite, i.e., infer about marital problems by examining some examples of global mentality. They clearly reflect the generality of social chaos and its impact on family mentality. We cannot ignore the global problems of nations fighting for their independence and self-determination. Ethnic struggles for separation from their motherlands, religious crusades, problems of the Middle East, and the Palestine's struggles to get back what Israel has captured as its own, are all reflections of who we are as human beings. It shows how our general attitudes toward others surface from our deep convictions and egoistic perception of 'us versus them.' The attitude that 'I know, I am good, but the rest are not' is the rule of our planet; a fact that we nurture and believe in very strongly. We always think we deserve more than the rest. Therefore, we draw a line to signify our borders, to isolate others and to keep everything for ourselves even if what we have is something we borrowed or captured by force from somebody else. It is ours now. It is difficult not to think of some Quebecer's struggle for sovereignty and independence from Canada. An image and expectation of being *distinct* from the rest of Canada gives them the incentive and stamina to fight for separation. What is behind this need for 'distinction' that drives us so blindly and forcefully in this journey of alienation? Has our disappointments from past human encounters and relationships brought us to such a non-reconciliatory position? Is it our inner urges pushing us so hard to prove our ability to be independent? Or, is it our egoism to prove our existence in the most retaliatory and controversial manner? These very same urges and forces that drive and convolute our social thinking and nationalistic struggles prevail in our personal lives too. In fact, they both are derived from the same source—egoism dictating our personal beliefs and needs. The prevalent forces that define and run our work habits and organizations are the same forces and Egos that run our marriages too.

Our selfish needs are reinforced by prevalent social values and 'generally-practiced' attitudes and expectations of other fellow humans. We reinforce each other's Ego to strive for foolish and unnecessary means of building and expressing our individualism, identity, and importance. The process of alienation in marital life is mainly influenced by these very same fundamentals of human nature and demented ways of thinking.

We get married with false expectations that are bound to fail anyway. We burden our marital relationships by so many demands and a haughty display of individualism, as if carrying the torch of separation from day one in our heads without realizing it. Even marriage itself is often considered only an exercise for separation from bachelorhood, which we feel is constricting our identity as someone who can (and must) be loved and needed. We think of marriage as an exercise to portray our individualism. We ignore that marriage is not a platform for expression of individualism and personal Ego or satisfying our personal needs. This mentality actually defeats the notion of developing personal independence. 'Individualism' requires humility and selflessness. Unfortunately, however, in society and marital life we interpret 'individualism' in a wrong way as a means of showing off our Ego and expressing personal power and abilities, whereas in fact the emphasis should be placed on teamwork and objectivity. Ironically, marriage is mostly a sign of our inability or unwillingness to be an independent individual! Most of us are too needy and soft to bear independence or grasp the true meaning of individualism.

Our initial, inflated expectations of marriage create the basic hurdles in building our relationships properly. Our first thoughts in marriage are about those things that we expect from our partners and all the great things that should now start to happen. We are unaware of marriage requirements. We have no vision of the demands on us to cope with the new way of life. We do not realize the sacrifices that are needed to stabilize our relationships and how our personal Egos must be managed more tightly to do that. We do not know or think about the responsibilities we must carry in a relationship and the delicate role we must play. Therefore, we do everything the wrong way by expressing a false personality in hopes of asserting our individuality and dominating the situation. Only when we learn the implications of an alienation journey, how it starts, and what triggers it, we may learn about the damaging roles we play in instigating alienation. We play a forbidding role when our attitudes and values make our partners feel alienated. And we play another negative role when our partners alienate us and we quickly resort to retaliation instead of dealing with the situation calmly and effectively.

CHAPTER SIX
Alienation Characteristics

SINCE alienation is the main road to separation, it helps to recognize its characteristics and prevent it from overtaking our relationships—before it is too late. We can beware of the symptoms of alienation that creeps up gradually in our marriage and destroys the relationship eventually.

Alienation is a *feeling* of dissociation with our partner and his/her ideas. It is a feeling of loss of influence on the direction of our relationship, and a lack of strength and motivation to do anything about it. We see our partner in a different light all of a sudden. Our new image of our partner is quite unfamiliar and cause internal unrest when we think about him/her. We feel as though we do not understand and know our partner. We do not grasp her/his logic and reasoning when analysing the facts of life and our marriage. No common ground exists for discussing our interests and needs, we do not trust his/her judgment, we feel falling more adrift from him/her every day, and we become more doubtful about our relationship. The level of intimacy appears to decline along with our respect for him/her, and we feel strange and uncomfortable in his/her presence.

In addition, alienation is a *state of mind* in which we give up arguing about issues and changes that we sought from our partner before. We prefer to stay passive and keep a distance from our partner in order to eliminate or reduce conflicts and arguments. We quit reasoning and often surrender to whims and desires of our partners, not because we agree with them, but rather because we doubt if our viewpoints have any value or effect. We feel emotionally defeated and exhausted by even the thought of approaching our partner to discuss or ask for something. We fear our partner and resent the arguments that may erupt at any point and any time we are together. We fear the games, blaming, nagging, and intimidations that usually erupt when we are together. Our contacts are unpleasant and therefore we try to minimize and control them.

Milder alienation trips start in our marriage before we get to the real alienation journey. We all walk on and off the alienation journey anytime we feel a sense of desolation or disappointment with our partners. The severity of conflicts rises only when we advance further out on this journey. Otherwise, mostly subtle and mild alienation trips set us off during our superficial and innocent arguments. Then, we usually return to our main journey of togetherness and cooperation. Nevertheless, while the effects of these alienation trips may be much less critical, so many trips—however short they may be—would eventually tire us and contaminate our relationship. Frequent trips eventually instigate the big journey of alienation.

Partners' depression naturally affects their sense of physical attraction and enjoyment. They engage in sexual relationships for lust rather than a feeling of love. The analogy of 'men going to their caves,' which John Gray has used in his book, is a reference to this alienation process. However, it seems that both men and women are equally moody from time to time and thus withdraw from their partners emotionally and physically on a cyclical routine. On some occasions, in fact, women show a higher tendency for withdrawal, especially during menstruation. The mood cycles are, nevertheless, reinforced when partners are on an alienation journey, however mild or subtle the alienation may be. Overall, men do not seem to 'go to their caves' more frequently than women considering the latter's natural tendencies and the effect of their hormones. Actually, it happens more to women also due to their higher emotional personality, for sensing and proving a higher need for autonomy these days, or perhaps for being from the planet Venus with a very peculiar mindset. In all, women are often more sensitive and demanding, and thus show a higher tendency to withdraw. There is a significant difference in the nature of withdrawals between men and women, though. Men's withdrawal is usually passive as they just hide in their shells. Women's, on the other hand, is usually showy, retaliatory, and spiteful. It may sound odd, but women's withdrawal could actually appear rather sneaky or diplomatic.

Several factors, including lower Model and higher Ego, make men more abrupt in their withdrawal, when their sense of alienation reaches its height temporarily. That is, when either men or women are on an alienation journey, perhaps even without realizing it, they would be inclined to keep a distance and avoid unnecessary contacts that would cause arguments. However, gradually the force of sexual needs begins to take over. At this stage, either men or women begin to crawl out of the cave and approach their partners for the eventual goal of satisfying their lust. Since men are usually more aggressive in (and less in control of) their sexual urges, their emergence from cave is more apparent and for the same reason their withdrawal might appear more transparent and crude. In all, the intensity of alienation sends both men and women to their caves according to genders' prominent personality aspects, and often their high urge for sex brings them out of seclusion.

Alienation makes partners see each other as aliens from different planets. They see and interpret things differently. They do not seem to relate to each other's viewpoints even when they try to explain or listen to each other. Sometimes, we think that our partner is resisting the opportunity to learn and s/he is deliberately fighting with our thoughts and opinions as well as the idea of cooperation.

Being from the planets Venus and Mars, we would expect men and women to see each other as aliens at the first sight. Thus, the fact that we initially meet so naturally and peacefully, fall in love, and express our intimacy and feelings toward one another so generously is puzzling and contradictory. This is how and why it becomes difficult to make a real judgment about the source and emergence of subsequent problems. If men and women are good and nice to each other at the beginning, then something makes them see their partner's real personalities after marriage so differently, in a way that had not been obvious before, or at least had felt more tolerable. Only partners' new perceptions, after marriage, result in partners seeing each other as aliens, if not enemies. Thus, it appears that men and women are from the planet Earth, after all, as they set out so naturally to get married and make woes and commitments to one another. However, every individual, man or woman, has different perspective of, and priorities in, life, which are not only unique, but also change all the time. Obviously, people are different in terms of their visions and aspirations. When these differences are not recognized as an inherent nature of human and we insist on equality and uniformity in all respects (including partners' intelligence level), then we get into trouble with our naïve expectations from marriage. And when the marital relationship is not bound by sensible guidelines and commitments, it falls into alienation traps easier due to our unclear and unfounded perceptions of marriage.

We may eventually get fed up with our marriage and think that time has come to separate. Before we reach this final point, we are usually aware of a process and a period of alienation. Yet, we often are not consciously aware of how we are travelling on this alienation path and then suddenly reach the end of the road and feel fed up. Or, we continue to live in a state of alienation for the rest of our lives without ever making the final decision to separate. The decision is hard, because we usually do not know where we stand in our relationship and cannot gather enough clues from all the signs that appear regularly on the alienation road. We are filled with huge doubts about our conclusions, relationship, and existence as a whole, and do not know how to deal with them.

Alienation Process

During an initial grace period after marriage, partners try to adjust to the new environment, routines, and expectations, and at the same time express (and assert) their views of marital life and plans. Partners test each other and try to prove themselves. They cleverly gauge their positions in the relationship and play with all aspects of their personalities to adapt, accommodate, express love, but most importantly mark their territories. Often a lot of passion and compassion is exchanged and they share common interests to increase their life enjoyments. The freshness of the experience allows partners forget all their other engagements and obligations temporarily to put the highest emphasis on the activities and conversations around their new life. Optimism and cooperation prevail and future looks bright and full of promises. Oh, how much we all miss that sweet period!

Soon, however, the reality kicks in and partners remember the importance of their other activities and responsibilities. They go back to their old habits and activities gradually, and accept marital life as a new foundation for accommodating all other activities and life objectives. Real life problems feel vivid and serious again, and thus the level of attention to our partner and his/her interests stabilize at a level that is convenient for us; not the level that our partner expects in his/her sensitive mind.

Strangely enough, while we balance the level of activities and attention to our partner's needs according to our needs and sense of practicality, we continue to expect our partner to give us the same level of love and attention that we need and imagined prior to marriage. We see our balancing act a practical move, but conceive our partner's adjustment a loss of his/her interest and thus a threat to our relationship. We start to doubt our partner's intentions, love, and commitment. Thus, we cultivate the first seeds of mistrust and alienation. Alienation is not serious at this point, but it deteriorates fast, unless partners learn to reconcile their mentality and activities with relationship requirements in the new era.

Both their own cooling down and their partner's adjusted attitude confuse both partners. The change and the confusion then lead to hurt feelings and reactions, openly or indirectly. Perhaps some hints and casual discussions of hurt feelings come up occasionally, each partner trying to justify his/her own intentions, but criticizing his/her partner's cooling attitude. Partners' quirks and anxiety start to surface in the form of insecurities, possessiveness, jealousy, withdrawals, etc., especially for couples who have relied too much on love to carry their relationships. Egos are usually under pressure and partners' frustration explodes in different ways. Their reactions set the pace for the next level of struggles. Hostile discussions and never-ending futile arguments make their lives miserable. Those who are less tolerant, or perhaps more practical in their minds, may give up already and ask for separation at this stage. However, the majority of us continue with our fights, arguments, and doubts, with hopes that someday our partner would understand our needs and demands and stop resisting our request to change.

We do not know that change is impossible even if our partner had all the best intentions to change. Nevertheless, the conditions continue to deteriorate, because we do not know how to handle the situation and soothe our injured Ego. We start to doubt the value of our arguments and the possibility of our partner caring for us enough to change, but we keep pushing him/her in different ways anyhow. Especially, if a mutual attraction exists, we continue to go through a cycle of arguments and fights - hostility and withdrawal - make up and sex - logical confrontation and justification - back to the beginning of the cycle - a new round of ferocious fights. However, every time we go through this cycle, a little bit of intimacy is scraped off our relationship. We lose confidence about our relationship and wonder whether our arguments would ever lead to any tangible results. We feel more alienated toward our partner and less interested to discuss the contentious issues. We start to doubt our decision to marry this odd person. Unfortunately, we find that the number of issues we avoid discussing rises gradually until there is really not much left to say to each other outside the very essentials, in a hostile tone.

However, we still do not give up. We are alienated somewhat, maybe a lot even. However, underneath all those doubts about the viability of our marriage and the fruitfulness of our struggles, some glimpses of optimism and hope keep us going. Both partners feel the burden of alienation and the heaviness of their silence, but neither dares or cares to initiate a conversation that would eventually stir more fights and disappointments. Both partners feel helpless in the depth of their doubts and despair, but alternatives do not seem promising either. Therefore, no attempt is made to do anything with the relationship but to tolerate it, for now at least.

The alienation grows gradually even with small and unintentional tactlessness, misunderstandings, and insensitive comments. Often, partners' idiosyncrasies expedite the alienation, usually in an early stage of marriage and proceeds hastily toward its final destination, as if we were travelling on a supersonic airplane rather than a sailboat. Obviously, the personality of partners, particularly their patience, affects the process and speed of alienation substantially. However, in effect, the final outcome and eventuality of separation do not change much if alienation reaches a point where return becomes insurmountable. If partners are so drastically different in personality and cannot find the means of cooperation to elude alienation, they are better off following the speedy process of concluding everything fast with minimal bloodshed. Long alienation journeys are suffocating and excruciating.

Innocent Causes of Alienation

Even minor personal idiosyncrasies and miscommunications cause alienation. A simple and subtle communication may be misunderstood and reacted upon antagonistically. Partners often raise old issues in hopes of clarifying a particular point better or solve an outstanding problem. Soon, however, this seemingly logical attempt makes them anxious, especially when the main topic of discussion vanishes in the midst of quarrels. For example, (A) innocently raises a particular old incident to demonstrate a general idea or perhaps a weakness in their relationship. However, (B) uses the occasion to argue about the relevance of the example and (A)'s hidden intentions to raise it again now. By itself, (A)'s example is meant to signify an event in the past, a life experience that might have some educational value. However, since (A) has brought up an old event, the argument is suddenly redirected toward a deeper marital problem. (A) is blamed again for his/her insensitivity, and s/he is dragged into a faultfinding exercise that leads only to more futile arguments.

In the early stages of marriage, especially, partners do not even understand the causes of their outbursts from simple points or observations, except that they get into lengthy arguments for matters that did not really matter anymore. They end up sleeping in different rooms and do not talk for perhaps a week or two with no substantive reason to support such childish behaviours. Finally, they may get a bit smarter and analyse their conversations and the causes of their conflicts and arguments. They may realize how they let their spouses drag them into needless and useless arguments based on simple conversations or an expression of their opinions, which has no direct relevance to, or importance for, their marriage. Eventually, partners may learn to avoid raising points that trigger fault-finding arguments about past events, which means they never give themselves a chance to learn anything from their experiences. The funny thing is that when a partner talks about a new issue, the other partner usually interrupts him/her and asks, "Like what? Give me an example." (Yet they both know better now that raising contentious experiences just open the can of worms all over again for a new round of arguments.)

Understanding simple conditions that trigger arguments and fights in marriage (such as the example noted above) does not mean that we can always avoid such explosive situations. Rather, this knowledge may raise our awareness of many conditions that often lead to miscommunication. The causes of miscommunications are numerous and unique for each couple. They, however, can make an effort to pinpoint those special topics or situations that trigger miscommunication. Strangely enough, often the causes of miscommunication are quite simple and mostly irrelevant to the issue at hand. They usually reflect the hidden problems and neglected needs of one or both partners, awaiting an opportunity to erupt. If not, it relates to the poor way each person handles the process of communication and how information is received, analysed, and reacted to. John Gray's book, *Men are from Mars, Women are from Venus,* Harpercollins; Harperperennial, 1992, refers to simple examples of miscommunication. Some of his examples are:

"Women say: 'We never go out',
men hear: 'You are not doing your job. What a disappointment you have turned out to be ... , you are lazy, unromantic, and just boring.',
they mean: 'I feel like going out and doing something together.'" Ibid., page 62.

"Women say: 'Everyone ignores me',

men hear: 'I am so unhappy, I just can't get the attention I need. Everything is completely hopeless. You should be ashamed. You are unloving.',

they mean: 'Today, I am feeling ignored and unacknowledged. Would you give me a hug and tell me how special I am to you?'" Ibid., page 63.

"Men say: 'I'm fine,' and

women hear: 'I don't care about what has happened. This problem is not important to me. Even if it upsets you, I don't care.',

They mean: 'I am fine because I am successfully dealing with my upset or problem. I don't need any help. If I do I will ask.'" Ibid., page 74.

These interpretations are not necessarily complete or always true, but they reflect how our miscommunications trigger our senses of insecurity and oversensitivity. Some interesting conclusions can, however, be deduced from these kinds of (mis)communications. First, they indicate that we hide our real needs and meanings in the context or tone of our communications. Second, we expect our partner to be sensitive and intelligent enough to understand and interpret our real meaning from all the miscommunications, moody attitudes, and hidden messages in our conversations. Third, we have become accustomed to this kind of incomprehensive communications and believe that it is appropriate. Fourth, it suggests that it is necessary to develop a sixth sense for interpreting our intentionally ambiguous communications and we should be blamed if our brain cannot learn to do so all the time. We have become too selfish to accept that miscommunication occurs because we express it in a strange and irrelevant manner, or simply because we are oversensitive or too demanding. Once we start this game (the process of miscommunication filled with futile hints and hidden expectations) between a couple, it would become a norm and normal routine for both partners to torture each other with their sarcastic, enigmatic communications.

Miscommunication occurs deliberately or innocently for many reasons. In particular, with the increase in individuals' stress level, preoccupation with a variety of tasks and problems, including personal and business priorities, the amount of time and patience necessary for communication never seems enough. We are constantly in a rush to go somewhere else and do something else and we expect our partner to know this. We expect our partners to not only understand our meaning in a communication even when it is not expressed straight, but also adjust his/her needs and communication style to accept and accommodate this kind of inordinate behaviour. The problem is that the more partners try to accommodate these kinds of infantile expectations, the more convoluted the communication norms become, and the more the chances of miscommunication and alienation get. We never seem to like to solve the depth of the problems, but only deal with their annoying symptoms *superficially*. These perfunctory solutions only create more confusion and stress, not to mention all the extra efforts that people must put into even their simple communications.

Couples feel alienated toward each other for many unintended and innocent gestures that get out of hand. We hurt each other with our passive/aggressive attitude and communication. We forget that our idiosyncrasies are responsible for inducing many miscommunications and alienating situations, directly or indirectly, with and without our intention. Of course, non-psychological and external causes of alienation also exist, like the effect of financial hardship, social norms, health issues, etc. However, the bulk of alienation problems are created because we are not aware and in control of our small flaws, including our persistence to use vague messages

and sarcastic tone for our communications. Some of the partners' idiosyncrasies that cause alienation are listed below:

The List of Alienation Causes

- Inability to communicate
- Miscommunication, intentional or due to carelessness
- Unwillingness or inability to share information and coop-
  erate
- Lack of trust or respect
- Deceit and insincerity
- Egoism and intimidation
- Lack of passion and compassion
- Personality clashes and incompatibility
- Insecurities and deprivation of personal needs
- Financial hardship, social pressures, and other external
  factors
- Unbalanced and unsatisfied expectations
- Perception of some or all of the above, especially the lack
  of love
- Etc.

Learning about the alienation process and its causes is important for detecting and acknowledging both our personal and
marital issues before it is too late. It can help us view marital
relationships more consciously as a dynamic environment
highly susceptible to (mostly self-induced) destructive alienation factors (as listed above). Nonetheless, we are personally
responsible for allowing these forces interfere and shape our
mentality and relationships. Self-awareness helps us recognize
the causes of alienation, adjust our attitudes and expectations,
and curb our debilitating habits that promote alienation.

Fighting Alienation

Normally, nobody imagines leaving his/her spouse when s/he is just getting married. We all *assume*, and imagine nothing but, a smooth and fruitful relationship developing gradually into a prosperous, happy partnership. This innocent assumption shows how things usually go wrong in spite of our good intentions. Of course, occasionally a partner changes his/her mind about marriage and thus actively causes alienation to get out of this commitment. When a partner is adamant about separation, no one and no advice can help the situation and partners.

However, alienation usually starts inadvertently against our good intentions. We prefer to stay married if external forces and partners' inherent quirks would allow it. Yet, always many things go wrong and alienation begins very early on in most marriages nowadays. Many individuals admit losing their marriage to their own sense of insecurity, which is only one common example of genetic deficiencies partners bring to their marital life and cause endless struggles. Therefore, we can search seriously for factors, mostly personal defects, that lead to our alienation after marriage.

Alienation is mainly a symptom of some real or perceived outside threat (mainly our spouse) provoking some of our psychological flaws, which we do not know about or cannot control. Usually, an external stimulus, e.g., our partner's flirting with someone else, provokes our hidden quirks. It triggers our sense of jealousy and insecurity beyond our control. In many situations, the external stimulus may not be even real. Rather, only our (mis)perception of external events often triggers our quirks. Our imagination can drive us crazy if we let it. And, of course, in many cases we become the subject of abuse by our partner without any fault or provocation on our side. We simply receive different kinds of abuse, perhaps even without our partner's direct intention to hurt or alienate us. Conversely, we may act in a way (intentionally or inadvertently) that provokes our partner. In this case, our action becomes an external stimulus for our partner whose reaction we observe and respond to (again) with another rude reaction of our own. Naturally, this series of actions-reactions can lead to further misperceptions, retaliatory exchanges, and of course alienation.

If partners are REALLY serious and sincere for sustaining their relationship, and only if they are not badly flawed beyond repair, they may be able to search for, and find ways of preventing, the causes of alienation. Hopefully, they can take some preventative measures against alienation process, though it is a difficult task. They must turn into much better persons than they are, to not only recognize and stop their alienating behaviours, but also learn to tolerate more hardship and psychological threats that usually persist in all marital relationships. However, by expressing and intending to be a 'good' and 'patient' person, we do not actually turn into one over night. It would take many years of conviction and faith to make it happen.

CHAPTER SEVEN
Alienation Preparedness

THE rather lengthy discussions in Part II of this book explain alienation, separation, and divorce dilemmas. Still, regretfully, the alienation process and its consequences are too complex and tricky to explain in one book. In all, the intention of this chapter, in particular, is to help readers gain enough knowledge about alienation preparedness process, learn how to apply the required steps properly to improve their relationships, and make the right decisions about their marital status.

Overall, the purpose of the 'alienation preparedness' process is to control the rotting relationship conditions that paralyse partners' judgment while they stagger and struggle on an alienation course. Through this self-awareness process, we also learn to make our judgments and decisions about marital problems only when we are in control of our thoughts and emotions, and not when we have lost our senses in the heat of arguments. We must remember that a judgment is sound only when it is free from prejudices, Ego, and heated emotions.

The Ultimate Options

We must ultimately make a conscious 'decision' about our relationships to mitigate our doubts and pains. Our ultimate options are to: i) stay in the relationship and continue to play an active role in defusing the alienation process, ii) stay in the relationship passively and patiently, or iii) separate. Option (ii) intends to make the best of the possible situation without making any further efforts to improve the conditions because of the continuous failures or partners' carelessness.

We try to choose one of these three options cautiously and *consciously* and then learn to live with its consequences. We face the same options with or without a valid judgment about the state of our relationship. With an objective judgment, however, we are convinced, committed, and play our roles with minimum doubts regarding the risks of the final decision and outcome. Hopefully, we make that tough decision calmly based on a valid judgment about the state of our relationship.

All three options are viable and wise choices depending upon the conditions of our relationships, our awareness of the depth and sources of our problems, and our past efforts in resolving the conflicts. Each option becomes applicable and most viable at some stage of our relationship, but our options become more restricted over time. That is, first we become aware and eager to resolve the problems. Next, we accept the problems as irresolvable and thus try to live with them without seeing any chance to improve the relationship. We choose a different relationship model that gives partners more independence within a rather passive relationship. And finally, we feel that the relationship is intolerable in spite of our efforts to correct or tolerate the situation, so we choose to separate. During these stages, we are forced involuntarily to travel fast on an alienation journey toward the separation destination. However, at the same time, we are struggling, with all our wisdom, conscious, conscience, Ego, Model, and Self to reverse the direction of the demised journey and return to the point of departure, where our relationship was meaningful.

Intuitively, all of us follow the same order of correcting, tolerating, and quitting our relationships whenever we have a marital problem. However, intuition would not help if it does not reflect a high level of awareness and patience. Our efforts would be productive only when we encounter these stages with full awareness, conscious, and conscience, according to an alienation preparedness process. Only then we get a better chance of resolving our problems, or at least finding a better means of controlling our doubts and making a valid judgment.

In all, it is unwise to jump to the second or third stages without fully exploring the opportunities that prior stages can offer. We should go through each stage with full awareness, patience, and valid judgment before making a decision to move on to the next stage. And within each stage, we should not hastily expect a sudden change and results, because most likely our awareness still needs expanding, and because the process of self-awareness takes a long time to perfect. If our aggravated Ego or emotions put us in the third stage quickly, without giving us the benefit of following an alienation preparedness routine, we are bound to make a major mistake that the whole family would suffer from and regret.

No right or wrong answer exists for the question of 'live or leave.' The only criterion is to ensure we make a *valid* judgment and a timely decision according to the ideas suggested in this chapter. The whole intention of alienation preparedness is to help us with this judgment and decision.

The importance of a separation decision calls for pondering many relationship issues and highlighting the implications of many crucial factors. A main point derived from our limited discussions is that, during a relationship crisis, we do not have the right mindset to judge and decide properly. Thus, we need an 'alienation preparedness' process, which encourages deep self-appraisal and self-awareness, to deal with ongoing crises and make fair judgments without letting egoism and emotions overwhelm our thoughts and senses in a stressful instance. We may go to marriage counsellors to help us make a decision, but nobody can help us without our genuine involvement, self-awareness, and a sound 'alienation preparedness' mentality.

Alienation Preparedness Factors

'Alienation preparedness' is just a precautionary antidote for marriage breakdown if partners have not drifted apart drastically. It is a preventative measure—vaccine—even if partners are already inflicted by the symptoms of alienation to some degree. With alienation preparedness, we plan to maintain the health of our relationships by:

1. Acknowledging potential relationship problems (as well as unique issues in any relationship)
2. Dealing with our psychological defects
3. Measuring and improving our tolerance
4. Recognizing our opportunities and fears
5. Admitting, planning, and playing our roles
6. Making objective judgments and decisions

Partners' perpetual attention to the above six steps, as personal responsibilities in relationships, is very important and thus briefly discussed in this chapter. In fact, when reading this book, especially this chapter, ask yourself whether both you and your partner have the patience and interest to study and use the issues discussed here. If not, the chances of alienation and failure are high for your relationship.

<u>Alienation Preparedness - Factor One</u>

Acknowledging Potential Relationship Problems

Unfortunately, we can no longer take our marriages as a *stable* support system (platform) for performing our more tangible duties and responsibilities of life. Most of our perceptions of marriage, especially about its stability, are flawed nowadays. We do not realize that marriage is an ongoing responsibility and challenge, for fulfilling special objectives, while partners must play specific roles properly and perpetually. We do not realize that the stability of marriage requires constant control and engagement. Even then, relationships remain forever quite vulnerable as a symptom of new social order and people's obsession for independence and identity. Unfortunately, relationships' stability was the luxury that old generations enjoyed so casually, but no more.

Similar to an earthquake, we can never anticipate the eruption of marriage turmoil. We can never foresee when one or both partners reach the end of their alienation journey so unexpectedly and their marriage tumbles under the pressures of alienation, as if a major earthquake had shaken the foundation and structure of their relationship. And similar to an earthquake preparedness program (to foresee and prepare for its severe repercussions), the 'alienation preparedness,' is merely a general plan to enhance our awareness about alienation and to learn how best to get ready to face and defeat it; or at least minimize its effects on ourselves and our family. Some general plans and guidelines are drawn in this chapter, but everybody can do his/her planning the best. Especially, recognizing partners' sensitivities and their marriage peculiarities gives everybody the best insight to prepare their astute and unique alienation preparedness plan.

The first step for 'alienation preparedness' is to study marriage environment, relationships' unique needs, and circumstances that often lead to alienation. Most of us take our marriages for granted subsequent to a short period of honeymoon, after our passion settles and we touch reality again. This does not necessarily mean that we lose our love or enthusiasm that fast. On the contrary, we feel secure and comfortable in our marriage environment. This gives us the psychological safety and a platform to ensue our life aspirations more actively. This is consistent with Maslow's theory, which speculates we move on to search and satisfy our higher needs once our lower needs (e.g., belonging and love) are satisfied. However, the problem is that we assume our marriage is as safe as we feel about our love and belonging needs. This may not be true. In fact, we have a wrong perception of marriage at the outset, as we assume that a normal (average) marital relationship would be problem free, despite all the stories and statistics that suggest otherwise. We assume marital problems emerge from those exceptional circumstances where partners are not normal or cannot handle their marital affairs logically. Thus, we see no reason to worry, since we consider both ourselves and our marital conditions *normal*. The problem with these assumptions is that nowadays even a 'normal' relationship gets entangled and tainted quickly by many complex circumstances because of the overall malfunctioning of social systems and partners' stress levels, misperceptions, and untamed expectations. There is no 'normal relationship' in society anymore. Thus, we must study and acknowledge three categories of information in our marital relationships:

i) Partners' compatibilities and quirks.
ii) Marriage environment, with the objective of learning about relationships' specific needs and keeping the peculiarities of our unique relationship at our conscious level permanently. We should also learn about different types of relationship models and determine which model best suits partners' personalities and needs.
iii) Main alienating factors in relationships and avoid them.

Grasping and acknowledging these three areas of potential problems in relationships keep us agile, as discussed below.

i) Acknowledging Partners' Compatibilities

Partners must know their areas and levels of compatibility before marriage, but also keep working on them forever. They could use the compatibility measures discussed in Chapter Three to do their own evaluation, or take some reliable tests that might become available. In particular, they must pinpoint their areas of incompatibility and avoid marriage, despite their attraction and love, if their incompatibilities seem excessive. Even moderate incompatibilities usually cause conflicts, so partners must learn about them and get ready to somehow deal with them effectively. In fact, more incompatibilities always emerge only after marriage, along with unexpected couples' eccentricities. Thus, partners should also be prepared for this possibility with open minds. They must learn to draw on the strengths of their compatibilities to offset the burdens of their incompatibilities and empower their relationship in general.

Acknowledging and applying partners' unique qualities for teamwork are especially important. The time and effort partners share for this exercise would by itself enrich their relationship. In most relationships, however, partners do exactly the opposite. That is, they waste their energies on finding each other's weaknesses to criticize in hopes of boosting their own Egos, manipulating each other, and controlling their relationship. They exhaust and depress each other, instead of recognizing, and benefiting from, their compatibilities or complementing qualities. They retaliate instead of acknowledge the need for teamwork and eliminating rivalry between partners. They ignore what they can offer individually to maximize the synergy in their relationship.

Obviously, if partners do not have enough areas of compatibility and unique personal qualities to offer, they should have not started their relationship to begin with. More importantly, if they have major or irreconcilable incompatibilities, they should not marry on the premise that their conflicts can be resolved or tolerated *somehow*. Nevertheless, the goal is to implement ideas and methods that promote their compatibility, while they stay alert about the areas of incompatibility, which demand partners' ultra attention and sensitivity. Learning to draw on their compatibilities is very important for bringing order into their relationship more consciously and actively and avoiding alienation.

After gauging their strengths and compatibilities, partners should eventually participate in objective (unbiased) evaluation of both partners' flaws and weaknesses, which often cause alienation—mainly due to partners' miscommunications and egoism. The focus is on personal flaws, however, in the sense that we try to resolve our own idiosyncrasies instead of finding our partners' and criticizing them. Alienation preparedness requires our conscious efforts to know and beware of the causes of miscommunication, as discussed in the last chapter (under Innocent Causes of Alienation) and in Chapter Eight.

Finally, partners must constantly be agile, and work on, their marital relationship as a routine practice of one's life. At this point, the task of awareness per se, is kept in partners' highest level of consciousness. The main objective is to keep ourselves abreast of our commitment to 'grasp marital needs and contentious problems.' Yet, this general awareness affects other aspects of our lives as well, including self-awareness. We can develop a 'marital awareness checklist' that reinforces our logic, purpose, impartiality, and awareness as a routine task for both cohabitation and self-development. Some items on this checklist may look like the following:

- Separation is mostly the outcome of an inconspicuous process of alienation that reaches a boiling (no-return) point unexpectedly.
- Alienation is a process that sneaks and grows gradually, so it must be constantly monitored with great diligence.
- Only partners' knowledge of the alienation process can prevent them from falling into this trap.
- Partners must play certain roles to alleviate or prevent alienation.
- Repercussions of alienation can be severe, even before it gets out of hand and leads to separation.

- Alienation is mostly caused by partners' psychological defects, yet misperceptions and miscommunications increase alienation fast.
- Many simple issues and judgments can cause alienation.
- Partners must be more conscious of the ways they convey, receive, and interpret their communication, including their tone of voice.
- Partners must be more careful in the ways their own oversensitivity and false pride may cause alienation and negative reactions.
- Without due sincerity, objectivity, and fairness, partners cannot stop the process of alienation.
- Etc.

ii) Acknowledging Marriage Environment

Partners must learn to view relationships as an independent entity with its own unique needs. In reality, however, everybody imagines that relationship needs must be an extension of their personal needs. They think that their relationships should satisfy a large variety of their personal needs and bring them happiness. This is a wrong expectation and assumption. In fact, it is the other way around. That is, partners are responsible for satisfying the specific relationship needs first, before it can fulfil even a few of partners' needs in any way. The topic of 'relationship needs' is quite extensive and readers are encouraged to study it in *The Nature of Love and Relationships* or *Relationship Needs, Framework, and Models*.

After learning about the unique relationship needs in general and committing to satisfy them, partners must also study the unique needs of their own relationship by paying attention to the details of partners' personalities, unique needs, sensitivities, aspirations, etc. They should understand what makes their relationships unique, both positively and negatively. The objective is to enhance partners' grasp of the critical issues and situations that cause concerns and misunderstandings between partners in their unique relationship. We want to learn about those irritating idiosyncrasies of partners that contaminate their relationship environment. The objective is to stay aware of their negative impact, and know how best to defuse them, while we learn about success factors in relationships, too.

In general, we must acknowledge that alienation can destroy our relationship environment, and then commit ourselves to some kind of alienation preparedness process to keep the relationship atmosphere open and peaceful. We admit that understanding the peculiarities of our unique relationship (and relationship needs in general) is not a casual exercise, but rather an ongoing commitment, responsibility, and condition. We then focus on relationship needs by discussing it with our partner on a regular basis, in a manner that both partners grasp and follow the purposes of alienation preparedness. It is important to share our thoughts and commitment with our partner for several reasons. First, by mere discussion of contentious issues (and alienation preparedness) we show our partner how serious we feel about our relationship and how patiently we must work together to pursue and exercise our *sensible commitment* to marriage. Second, dialogue per se enhances friendship and teamwork. And finally, through dialogue we may be able to raise our partner's interest about the benefits of 'alienation preparedness' and perhaps joining in with us to make it a permanent facet of our relationship.

As our main task for developing a relaxed relationship environment, we must establish 'how much we care' about our marriage, and admit our fear of alienation destroying our relationship. Simply, we must become sincerely committed and admit the importance of a serene relationship environment before it loses its momentum on an alienation course. Yes, relationships must have and maintain a momentum rather than being left alone to dry out or get sluggish. Knowing the consequences of alienation can help us focus on the task of finding out 'how much we care.' Still, we often have some doubt about 'how much we *really* care.' We have doubts about the quality and viability of our marriage.

Worst of all, we have doubts about 'how much we care about our spouse.' We know that we care about him/her, but we do not know 'how much.' We do not have a standard for measuring our level of 'caring.' Therefore, we often trust our emotions, which are either too soft or hard, but also tentative and driven based on our recent perceptions of our partner. We do not know how our 'caring' can, or should, translate into a measure of tolerance of our partner's defects.

We often gauge our 'caring about our partner' intuitively by comparing him/her with people we really love, like our children or parents. Accordingly, our spouse usually gets a low score on that scale, which then heightens our doubts about our level of caring for him/her, the purpose of our relationship, and our options. Especially for people who crave love keenly, their mediocre caring about their partner usually feels inadequate and a cause for concern. We always crave to love someone and also be loved. However, real caring is different from, and does not necessarily requires, love. Anyway, the more partners realistically care for each other, the more actively they care about keeping their relationship atmosphere peaceful.

Usually when couples separate temporarily because one partner goes on a long trip or perhaps lives alone after a fight, they get a chance to figure out how much they care about each other and their marriage. Then again, we do not know whether this caring, during our partner's absence, is our reaction to loneliness or passion for our partner—perhaps a little bit of both. This knowledge is valuable not only for the information it provides about 'how much we *really* care,' but mostly because it encourages us to learn 'why we care,' by measuring the *content and features* of our relationship. We must know

why we care about the health of our relationship with this particular person.

After we learn 'how much we care and why,' we like to establish 'how much our partner cares.' This is even a harder
task because it is difficult to imagine what goes on in our partner's mind. Even when our marital relationship does not seem
to work, most of us still give our partner the benefit of a doubt
and find all sorts of excuses to justify his/her random displays
of carelessness. (This is because we wish to believe that we
are still being loved and lovable. And sometimes because we
need him/her so badly.)

On the other hand, some of us are usually overly pessimistic about the health of our relationships. We interpret our partner's slightest impatience and neglect a sign of apathy and
carelessness. Then this misunderstanding affects our image of
our relationship and partner. However, many reasons might
exist for our partner's seeming carelessness. We can try to find
out the truth behind the appearances, i.e., his/her actions and
behaviours, if we care. Nonetheless, for pursuing our 'alienation preparedness' objective, we must initially establish
whether both partners genuinely care for each other and their
relationship, regardless of what their words and appearances
may suggest.

Another important factor to learn regarding relationship
environment is that different types of relationship models are
becoming prevalent nowadays to fit our modern lifestyles and
odd personalities. It is wise to study these models and adopt a
suitable one according to partners' personalities. Instead of
dreaming about an ideal relationship that satisfies all the needs
and aspirations of both partners, usually a more liberal relationship model, where partners have higher independence, can
minimize alienation and increase the health of a relationship.
Discussions about relationship models are also extensive and
thus readers are encouraged to learn more about this topic in
The Nature of Love and Relationships or *Relationship Needs,*

Framework, and Models. Overall, the idea is that, with the higher independence of partners, their expectations from their relationship are reduced and thus partners would not interfere with each other's personal affairs or get on each other's nerves too much all the time.

Naturally, it would be difficult to improve a relationship very much without both partners' cooperation and while one of them is highly careless. However, it would be even harder to interpret the meaning and purpose of our partner's apathy about our relationship and the ensuing alienation. His/her indifference feels like a major blow in our face any time we attempt to assess the flaws of our relationship. It may be a sign of her/his indifference toward us and our ideas of any kind, including awareness exercise and alienation preparedness.

Often one or both partners remain careless because they do not know how to go about discussing relationship needs calmly and objectively. Sometimes, our partner may appear careless because s/he has lost faith in our abilities to reconcile our differences, or perhaps s/he has even lost interest in our marriage altogether. S/he might have lost his/her trust in, and respect for, us. However, apathy may be a sign of internal frustration, as her/his efforts to prevent alienation do not seem to be effective, perhaps because we are not responding favourably to her/his efforts to fight alienation, or because we do not understand his/her approach or meaning.

Carelessness may be a sign that our alienation has grown beyond repair. It can also be only a mask, a Model presentation, for a partner's hidden inner turmoil and conflicts. S/he may be angry, jealous, or insecure about the events that surround our relationship, but plays a careless role in order to protect his/her Ego or to avoid unnecessary quarrels. Sometimes, showing indifference is merely for drawing the partner's attention to oneself or toward unresolved relationship conflicts. Thus, the trick is finding the right cause of our partner's

apparent apathy, which might include one or more of the possibilities noted in these pages.

Another scenario may be that our partner cares enough
about our relationship, but does not feel necessary, or does not
have time, to get involved in alienation preparedness routines.
Of course, if we can convince him/ her to join and share the
responsibility for alienation preparedness, the chance of success increases exponentially. However, this may prove to be a
frustrating challenge. On the other hand, if we constantly face
our partner's resistance to participate, we must eventually decide personally whether and how to fight alienation alone. By
the mere fact that our partner does not show any cooperation
or share responsibility for enhancing our martial relationship,
we are forced into a state of isolation and alienation. However,
that is not necessarily a reason to give up yet.

It is possible that our partner has already reached his/her
conclusions. Maybe s/he thinks we have already travelled so
far on our alienation journey that discussing marital problems
would not help. Sometimes, one partner does not talk about
his/her concerns and expect the other to understand her/his
meanings automatically and perhaps even show some kind of
concession. And sometimes, the excuse for his/her silence is
that s/he is not listened to, or cared about, or that their communication often leads to arguments and useless fights. Nevertheless, when a partner refuses to discuss his/her views, the
process of mutual awareness is hindered. To understand the
depth of our problems and assess the process of alienation,
however, we eventually need to receive our partner's reactions
and feedback for gauging our position.

Our partner's seeming disinterest to participate actively in
the process of awareness and alienation preparedness confuses
us. It is frustrating to keep guessing various reasons for it. Is
s/he quiet because s/he is agreeing with some of our suggested
solutions and thus silently and gradually changing her/his attitude and approach? Is it because s/he is not willing to accept

our suggestions out of spite, or only trying to avoid giving us a reason to brag about how right or smart we are? Is it because s/he is careless inherently and we are wasting our time and breath? Is s/he in complete disagreement, but afraid to say so because of possible retaliation? Or, because s/he simply does not want to get into arguments and useless awareness efforts? Would not s/he have become more enthusiastic and spoken up already if our efforts were working? May be yes, may be no. Nevertheless, making both partners believe in the *value of alienation preparedness* for keeping a peaceful relationship environment is ideal, but often unrealistic.

We normally emphasize the importance of communication for keeping the relationship atmosphere open. However, in fact, the underlying *awareness* property of communication makes it so important and mostly for preventing alienation. Communication without the objective of 'learning and acknowledging' would be mostly a waste of time and a cause for more arguments and conflicts (which is another form of losing sight of relationship unique needs).

Sometimes, communication is merely for the sake of creating joyful moments to share with our partner. A more important aspect of it, however, is to encourage and develop a relaxed environment while partners enhance their awareness about themselves and their relationship. Conversely, if partners communicate with the objective of 'raising partners' awareness,' their relationship environment improves drastically too. For example, one-way communication to only listen to our partner's concerns and needs can be considered an awareness-oriented exercise. However, we must understand the gist of the information we receive through listening to our partner's words. Our communication should have some useful content and objective. We should try to grasp the root of his/her concerns. Are our Ego, insensitivity, and careless attitude hindering the sincerity of our relationship? Or, is it those unfounded demands and whining of our spouse that make us alienated and unable to really communicate? Often, it is a combination of both. Or, perhaps the mechanism of communication, so far, has been weak and caused these side effects.

iii) Acknowledging Alienating Factors

Many factors start an alienation process, but the tentative list presented on page 96 is useful for pinpointing the areas of potential problems in most relationships. Some events, situations, and behaviours in any marital relationship usually point to one or more of these main alienation factors plus a variety of smaller issues. Together, these sources of alienation complicate the mood and content of a relationship beyond all the standards that partners had imagined. Partners get confused, lose track of their problems, and sometimes quarrel over trivial matters that have no effect on their relationship even if they were resolved. Partners find something else to nag about all the time. Deep down, they are often quite apprehensive about many irreparable conditions and do not like to even think about them, e.g., their loss of respect for their partner.

A seemingly small irritant may in fact reflect a major problem, while some of partners' naggings may be only small excuses to hide major problems in their personal lives or relationships, e.g., when one partner is having an affair. Nonetheless, studying even small incidents can help us learn more about the deeper issues in a relationship. Even small arguments may indeed be symptoms of one or more larger problems hidden or ignored all along, most likely because partners have had difficulty in finding a solution for them. At the same time, even unresolved small problems can gradually turn into a major alienation factor in a relationship. Through awareness, partners might learn to become more sensitive about the issues requiring emphasis, and making less fuss about intangible ones.

Some problems are quite overwhelming and we simply cannot face them, so we ignore them, hoping they would go away by themselves. Meanwhile, we continue to suffer the consequences while approaching marriage breakdown, too, because we refuse to take a positive action. For example, a gambler or alcoholic has a major problem without him/her admitting to it, or worrying about its consequences on his/her marriage until it is probably too late to do anything about it. The difficulty lies in pinpointing the main problems that demand immediate attention from amidst the bulk of trivial problems. Often, we create many other problems for ourselves and our partner just for avoiding the main one. We waste most of our time and energy on faultfinding, retaliation, and creating new problems for each other. Thus, we hardly get any impetus and motivation to deal with those few major problems of a relationship. When our minds are preoccupied by blames and demands all the time, we find no incentive or creativity to work on solving the main problem.

Again, we should remember that 'alienation preparedness' is an ongoing process. It evolves in small steps and results in incremental wisdom about our relationship and ourselves. We cannot expect to identify the main problem(s) and become aware of the circumstances and flaws of our relationship quickly. Rather, we can find better explanations and solutions for our alienation problems only by spending time and efforts to learn about the intricacies of all relationships. We also learn about the demands and needed resilience to pursue the learning process objectively and gain the required wisdom to save our marriage.

Once the main problem(s) are identified and brought into a high level of consciousness, our tensions would subside, even though the problems are not resolved yet. Just the mere knowledge about the real source of relationship conflicts relieves a great burden from our shoulders and reduces the stress caused by confusion and a sense of helplessness. It would be more productive if both partners agreed on the source of their problems. Just by mere concentration on major problems, we become creative in finding solutions, or configuring the hidden causes of problems. We realize that usually a mix of major and minor issues causes complications, conflict, and alienation.

Studying alienating factors in relationships often points toward partners' unique psychological defects, which are discussed in the next section. However, a typical situation, which usually leads to conflicts and alienation between couples, is when partners go through a period of cool down—may be a few days of withdrawal—before a specific or subtle mechanism brings them back together. Most often partners' sexual urges push them to reconcile. One partner usually takes the first step, though, not based on who feels guiltier or in need of sex, but rather his/her psychological vulnerability during that specific period. On the other hand, a partner may have a stronger, forgiving personality and thus initiate reconciliation. Accordingly, a sense of power struggle and relative domination seem to prevail in almost all relationships. Perhaps it is not intentional, but this inhibiting condition contaminates almost all relationship atmospheres somehow.

Partners' psychological vulnerability fluctuates according to their daily experiences. For example, when a partner is unemployed, struggles with office or health problems, etc., s/he feels mentally weaker than normal. His/her depleted confidence and need for affection make him/her vulnerable to all kinds of abuse and manipulation. During such times, this partner is usually subdued and eventually forced to initiate the makeup process after every fight or even small conflicts. This approach eventually leads to resentment about self for being such a loser. Conversely, one partner may wish to have everything under his/her control, to the extent that s/he may even create a fight only to humiliate his/her partner, just for enjoying his/her partner's defeat and maybe even getting a direct apology. S/he is usually attempting to justify and affirm his/her position about their marital conflicts while refuting his/her partner's viewpoints.

Only through alienation preparedness process, partners may realize that these games and approaches are unfair, and how they may ruin their relationship. They might develop a sense of fairness and learn to become less dogmatic for reconciling their regular skirmishes. They do not even need to agree on a mechanism for reconciliation, as it would happen automatically while grasping the intricacy of their relationship. The main objective, of course, is to disallow a variety of inevitable conflicts between partners linger too long and lead to alienation.

The best reconciliation mechanism is when partners try to use a combination of taking turns and using their conscience to initiate a makeup after going through a cool-down period. The trick is to realize and respect each other's equal needs for building and maintaining their confidence and self-image for (and through) their relationship. Through 'alienation preparedness,' partners learn to boost each other's confidence rather than taking advantage of a partner's diminished spirit at a specific time. They realize how humiliating it is for a vulnerable partner to become also a subject of his/her partner's carelessness and blackmail.

The above noted simple cases prevail in many relationships, but partners are not quite aware of them or do not know how to deal with them. The sad reality is that our own psychological needs and insecurities cause these small problems or misunderstandings and quickly turn into fundamental sources of alienation.

Alienation Preparedness - Factor Two

Acknowledging Our Psychological Defects

After acknowledging the severity of potential relationship problems, the next step in 'alienation preparedness' is to acknowledge our personal idiosyncrasies, which often taint our relationships. The main objective is to 'deal with our psychological flaws,' but also acknowledge that everybody is loaded with defects. Our imaginary standards of human beings in terms of intelligence and morality vastly surpass their instincts and nature. We imagine ethics much better than we can ever attain it as a human. Only when we accept that nobody is even half-perfect as our Ego suggests, or our Model pretends, we can proceed to better ourselves as a person and a companion, exude more compassion, and prevent alienation.

We must go through a rigorous awareness process to learn about our defects, understand who we are, and gauge the personality that portrays us to others. We learn that, for the most part, our psychological defects are neither created nor controlled by us. Therefore, acknowledging them is not intended to cause shame and guilt in our minds. On the contrary, merely our persistence to ignore them shows our naivety and arrogance. We should be only ashamed of, and feel guilty about, our stubbornness, and sometimes our inability, to accept the universality and depth of human imperfections. We all still have a hard time grasping the essence of our being—our nothingness.

Through soul-searching and self-assessing, we might finally grasp the depth of our psychological defects, and then learn to what extent we wish to control them or let them control us. We need enough maturity to gauge these defects and their impacts on our and other people's lives. We always resist criticism and change, as we believe we are perfect already, and that we know everything about ourselves and everybody else. This basic psychological barrier hinders our search for wisdom and tranquility. We are addicted to certain lifestyles and our false personality, and thus resist the notion of becoming a more natural and purer person, which we believe we can never be nor see any reason to be. This is like expecting a chronic smoker give up smoking because he knows the hazard of his habit. Perhaps assuming that we are not necessarily aiming for changing ourselves, at least not initially, eases our natural resistance to discover the deeper aspects of 'self' and who we really are. Detecting our defects does not create an automatic commitment for change, though our new knowledge of self may lead to a gradual transformation from within without too much effort to bring change about.

We must pinpoint our personality aspects that dominate our relationship with our partner. That is, we must try to establish how we relate; how much of our contacts and relations are driven by Ego, Self, or Model. Especially, when a good portion of partners' demands and attitudes are Ego driven, they may learn how, and how much, they are contributing to the demise of their relationship. They should be fair and unbiased when reviewing their attitudes and roles in undermining each other. Similarly, they must become aware of their partner's prominent personality aspects and understand how they might cause more alienation and less opportunity to reconcile.

It is naturally harder to see and accept our own defects than those of others because of the way our Ego stands in the way, and in the manner we set personal standards of normal behaviour unilaterally. We are selfish in the way: i) we truly believe that whatever we do is right and justified, ii) we use our self-serving beliefs and standards to set standards and judge others with prejudice, and iii) we use double standards for ourselves and others shamelessly. We impose double standards when we use one criterion to judge ourselves or someone we like, and use a different criterion for judging others, especially our adversaries. We are hardly aware of our quirks. When, on occasions, we notice some clues of our wickedness and weaknesses, we find ways to suppress our thoughts and intentionally support our defective perception of life and our role in the midst of it all.

Nevertheless, we can at least learn that our psychological flaws comprise of, i) those we simply cannot see, and ii) those that we face from time to time, but deliberately send to our unconscious swiftly in order to justify whatever we wish to do without a sense of guilt and remorse. Even this basic awareness might make us more conscientious and conscious of who we are. Meanwhile, our psychological flaws continue to cause great sufferings for others and us, as long as we remain not serious or compassionate enough to do something about them. By acknowledging our own and humans' natural flaws we can i) heal our obvious flaws, ii) deal with our partner's defects, and iii) remember the wide scope of simple psychological flaws that cause alienation.

i) Healing Our Obvious Flaws

If motivated to do anything about our psychological flaws, we can start with those we already know about and face regularly. For example, our sense of rivalry, jealousy and selfishness are not too difficult to spot in our feelings and dealings with others. We can remember these flaws in our conscious mind and witness them appear and interfere in our relationships and decisions regularly. By remembering them, we can tame these defects a bit, though we cannot get rid of them completely. We normally find an excuse to abandon our chances for learning. We quickly forget our commitment to monitor and assess our behaviour in an unbiased way. For example, if we are jealous, we blame it on our partner who instigates it in us.

It feels more natural to us to control others—in this case our partner who makes us jealous—than to control our own defects. For one thing, we consider our partner's behaviour provocative, which raises our doubts about his/her intentions or innocence. Is s/he a devil or merely a gullible? Since we cannot control our doubts (or misperceptions) about her/his intentions, we try to control the source of our doubts and provocation—our partner. After all, if we did not doubt our partner's intentions, we would not be suffering about everything s/he does. Anyway, regardless of her/his intentions, wicked or innocent, we feel the urgency to deal with the cause of our suffering in the quickest way—by controlling our partner. As another obstacle for learning about our defects, some of them—e.g., competition and greed—have become such a prominent part of our personality nowadays, they manifest as fully inherent and normal behaviour beyond our control. Heck, the whole society propagates them as valid norms. Thus, we manipulate and hurt others in different ways, e.g., through rivalry or out of greed, instead of acknowledging the personal defects we seem unable to control.

Many of these so-called norms (defects) are, however, reversible habits acquired through social conditioning. Our life experiences, humans' cruelty, and the prevailing unfairness, sometimes even by destiny and God Himself, make us cynical and callous. Yet, our seeming helplessness against our defects is not completely true.

Although receiving professional help is wise, we should mostly depend on ourselves to learn about our defects. Realizing our obvious defects and those still hidden, and our chance of defeating them eventually, but gradually, we can strive to find the strength in our psyche to control and turn things around. The only trick is to believe in our inner power and the possibility of drawing upon it once we become sincere to detect our deeper flaws.

The significance of our attempt to learn about our defects and do something about them is in *the way* it improves the quality of our relationships. Conversely, our relationships offer a good setting to explore our defects, while we can test our new convictions in the way we relate to others less selfishly.

We learn about not only our defects, but also their effects on others, especially those people we seemingly care for. Thus, we learn about caring and showing compassion too. This would be the beginning of a self-cleansing and soul-searching endeavour, which brings higher value and rewards beyond the basic benefit of controlling our defects.

The way we would eventually view and judge our defects, and subsequently the defects of others, would be significant. Instead of blaming ourselves and others and paining everybody in the process, we view our psychological defects as a mirror of past experiences that we can try to break through in order to enter a healthier lifestyle beyond our existing routines. We can view our struggles to defeat our defects a healing process, which may expand our lives and thoughts to such magnificent planes beyond common imagination. In fact, we could take a negative aspect of our lives and turn it into an exercise of tranquility and beauty. How easy it is to grasp the meaning of real life, and yet how difficult we have made it for ourselves to even appreciate the divinity we can attain by defusing our simple defects like Ego. We can forgive ourselves instead of merely ignoring our defects. Once we focus on forgiving instead of forgetting our defects, the process of healing begins.

Acknowledging our most obvious flaws, and their direct impacts on our minds and souls, also provides a good chance to test our willpower and wisdom. Mitigating those direct and constant sources of our suffering, such as rivalry and greed, gives us enormous strength and tranquility to challenge the deeper and less obvious flaws. The awareness of our defects, and our attempts to control them, avails the opportunity to find out more about our 'self' and learn to live within its boundaries more naturally. Accordingly, our new wisdom and vision of our 'self' makes the alienation preparedness process smoother and easier.

Acknowledging our defects does not threaten our identity or raise our psychological insecurity, contrary to what our challenged Ego wants us to believe. It only opens a window of opportunity to observe our inner hurts and insecurities and delve into our more complex nature after working out our most common and obvious flaws. Thus, we gradually get into the deeper aspects of our psyche and explore our 'being' and, in the process, encounter the devil that stands between what we are and what we want to be. We would also find the courage to accept input from our spouse on any flaws that s/he can see, but have remained hidden from us. By the strength of our soul, we would stop rejecting the information that flows readily through people's view of us and about how we hurt others. We would welcome the information because we now have ways of assessing its viability and value to us without getting offended and defensive. We listen to people's comments open-mindedly, although they may be, and often are, wrong.

ii) Dealing with Our Partner's Defects

Only after acknowledging the depth and implications of our defects sincerely, we are ready to assess our partner's psychological flaws. However, now our assessment of his/her flaws is merely a compassionate exercise and vision, as debilitating factors largely outside of his/her control. We start by recognizing that our partner also has two types of flaws. The ones s/he somewhat knows about and the ones that s/he does not realize. Our basic challenge is to acknowledge our inability to do anything about our partner's flaws directly. We can do something about ours, but not his/hers. Thus, our view of his/her flaws is only for the sake of 'alienation preparedness,' and for helping us gauge our ability to cope with them while we wait for a natural transformation in her/him (which may happen only rarely under certain circumstances through personal life experiences). Instead of blaming and trying to change our partner, we now become more understanding of people's difficulty in controlling their flaws. We can play a role—as will be noted shortly—but our expectations are different from what we have had before awareness. Our awareness is only for re-examining our expectations in marriage and controlling our anger and anxiety. Thus, we suffer less personally, cause less sufferings for our partner, and find more energy to take pro-ductive initiatives that often produce the same results we were after in the first place—i.e., when we were struggling hard to change our partner to accommodate our needs.

Knowing the type and extent of our partner's shortfalls and their impacts on us is useful *only* for improving our judgment and tolerance level. The goal is to become fairer and more ob-jective in our judgment about her/his intentions and control over his/her attitude. This knowledge can help us mitigate our doubts about the viability of our relationship and build toler-ance, at least for a short while, without always making a big issue quickly out of our partner's conflicting personality and flaws. The question is how much efforts are required on our part to live with relationship flaws without blaming or arguing with our partner about them indefinitely. That is, since s/he cannot change, how much time are we willing to devote to saving our relationship before asking for separation? The next question is whether we have played our role properly to miti-gate alienation. If there is, in our minds, any time that we can spare to view things from a different perspective, before ask-ing for separation, then that may be the most productive time in our marriage, hopefully.

With our new approach in dealing with our partner and her/his flaws, s/he notices our 'attitude change.' This would be a basic positive step in reversing the process of alienation. By not nagging at or criticizing our partner, s/he would put down her/his guard. Then, we use our energy to appreciate the new opportunity opening up in our relationship. S/he would try to figure out what has made us change our attitude and approach. This would provide a chance to use the one-way-a-time communication method or similar mechanisms to voice our concerns logically without pressing our expectations or asking him/her to change. We would only talk about our concerns and issues that hurt us or weaken our relationship. Our change of attitude and rising patience most likely show in our sincere, diplomatic approach automatically.

As noted above, we can do certain things about our partner's defects without aiming to change her/him. We can *indirectly and tactfully* raise our partner's awareness about his/her psychological defects, the impact they may have on our relationship, and how they are reinforcing the alienation process. We do this in different ways. For the most part, what we show by our non-blaming and patient attitudes would lead to positive reactions, in most people, in due time. REAL patience implies (and may require) waiting for some months or even years before its significance can be established in our spouse's eyes. Yet, this level of awareness and patience (waiting) by itself would change us and our expectations anyways in terms of viewing and handling relationship conflicts. Thus, even some minor compromises by our partner starts to appear pleasing and quite noticeable. Then, with our subtle acknowledgement of his/her efforts would come more tangible changes, because s/he would find them satisfying and rewarding, compared with the old method of demanding and expecting.

While working with our partner to mitigate the effects of our flaws, we might notice the positive changes and progress in each other's attitudes. Giving feedback to each other about noticed improvements would be helpful. Most improvements are probably insufficient, but still a move in the right direction. They should be acknowledged and encouraged, so that partners realize that they have understood each other and have intended to do something about their irritating habits. Waiting for an ultimate result before giving feedback and encouragement to our partner would cause further alienation. This is because our partner is doing his/her best to overcome some of his/her defects, which is a very difficult task to accomplish. His/her efforts per se are valuable even though the result may not be apparent for a long time. Partner (A) would perceive (B)'s lack of feedback a sign of (B)'s carelessness or a sign of (A)'s futile efforts to change, which seem to have no tangible outcome on their relationship. We do not have to get into a formal expression or appreciation of the improvement. In fact, doing that may have adverse effect on some people. Rather, we should give our feedback by implied gestures of appreciation and perhaps an emotional reward as simple as a warm smile in a proper moment, or an invitation to a romantic dinner at the right mood and time. Then, making some hints, maybe indirectly, can help too.

Our efforts help us directly, and we can help our partner indirectly by our attitude, but also by introducing her/him to alienation preparedness process when s/he seems ready to listen to our experience. The ultimate success comes when both partners begin to trust each other's judgments about their personal and relationship's weaknesses, especially the ones causing their alienation. This would help them recognize their less obvious flaws gradually and overcome their doubts and hesitation to admit them. We cannot necessarily get rid of our defects because we have acknowledged them. Both partners know that and take this barrier into consideration in their dealings and expectations from each other. However, the mere attention to our flaws, especially knowing that our partner is also aware of his/hers and acknowledges them, at least slows the process of alienation, and instead transcends us to a level of understanding and compassion, then the healing, and finally the effective control of personal flaws.

iii) Simple Psychological Defects

Fortunately, the psychological defects of majority of us are not too extreme to require specialized attention and cure. We are mostly inflicted with small and simple defects. However, unfortunately, these simple defects, such as lying, deceit, rivalry, and greed, have become an inherent part of our personalities and manifest in our dealings through Ego and Model. They are deep, negative personal traits and emotions that occur excessively, like the ones listed in the 'Simple Psychological Defects' box of Table 7.1 in the next page.

It is easy to conceive how one or more of the simple personal flaws noted in Table 7.1 can turn into many factors of alienation. Of course, an alienation situation has other causes besides psychological defect too. For example, a misunderstanding or a partner's weakness in expressing him/herself can create miscommunication, although they are not psychological flaws. Yet, even small weaknesses may lead to deep alienation issues.

Table 7.1: Personal Defects Causing Alienation

Simple Psychological Defects	Causes (Factors) of Alienation	
• Anger, spite, nagging • Insecurity, jealousy, possessiveness • Narrow perception of the world • Wrong objectives of life, greed, rivalry • Suspicion, insecurity, fear, pessimism • Lying, deceiving, dishonesty • Self-centredness, arrogance, meanness • Extreme obsessions • Etc.	> >	• Inability to communicate • Miscommunication • Unwillingness or inability to share/cooperate • Lack of trust • Deceit and insincerity • Lack of love • Ego/intimidation • Incompatibility & personality clashes • Need Deprivation • Financial issues • False perceptions • Etc.

> Alienation

Mentioning a real story about weakness in communication may help here. It happened when a woman asked for her partner's help. One Sunday morning, an unexpected snowfall covered the streets and driveways. He is in the middle of a job when his wife interrupts him and asks about his plan to shovel the snow in the driveway.

It is around one p.m., snow has stopped, and it seems to him that it may rain and clean the snow in the driveway. He looks at her with surprise and asks her "Why?" The wife replies, "Because we have to go to work tomorrow! If you don't, it might freeze overnight and make the driving out of the garage difficult in the morning."

To avoid needless arguments, he agrees, "Yes, ok. I will do it later this afternoon." Only when she leaves the room with stress, he realizes the weakness of his communication. Without telling her his reasons, his wife did not have any clue why he was resisting the idea of helping her, so she took it as a blunt rejection. He could have instead said, "Yes, I will. But let's wait for a couple of hours to see if it will rain and clear the snow." Sometimes, we try to economize in our communication, or assume our partner can read our minds. Thus, a simple weakness of communication can cause major, lasting misunderstanding for both partners, which can easily lead to further retaliatory actions and arguments.

On the other hand, we do not always have a presence of mind and excellent communication skills to be as precise in our interactions as is needed to avoid misunderstanding. Even if we did, it would be too exhausting and time-consuming to be precise with all our communications. Therefore, we should always think that what we hear and understand from our partner's comments is most likely not all the facts that s/he had meant to convey. We should ask for clarification calmly when the message is not clear enough to us or sounds weird.

Alienation Preparedness - Factor Three

Measuring and Improving Our Tolerance

Without great tolerance and patience, we do not last long in a marriage. Most of us learn this fact the hard way eventually. What we perhaps do not fully recognize, however, is that _high_ 'tolerance' is an inevitable reality of marriage, a general rule—an absolute necessity. Rather, we perceive tolerance as a major sacrifice and inconvenience (maybe torture) that only we endure. We are actually becoming less patient and tolerant in our relationships due to our misperceptions about the purpose of marriage, obsession for individualism and love, and stress from our other life responsibilities. Moreover, we have doubts about the definition and level of tolerance that can be considered normal and practical in a marital relationship. These doubts often increase impatience (and intolerance) all by themselves.

The other problem is that we mostly depend on our Ego to decide on the tolerance level that feels normal to us. Usually, during arguments with our partner, not only our offended Ego becomes in charge of viewing, analysing, and tackling the issues, but also we depend on this very impatient and selfish aspect of our personality to decide on how much more we can (or should) tolerate the situation. Thus, we hurry for separation and divorce, get entangled in an alienation process, find ourselves a lover, spend most of our time with friends doing things away from our spouse and family, get dissolved in too much work or personal hobbies, etc.

Thus, a main test for a couple contemplating marriage is to gauge their tolerance level very carefully and remember that without high tolerance no marriage survives these days. If partners are not mentally and logically prepared for this basic need of relationships nowadays, they should avoid that marriage at all cost, even despite their great love. Partners must know how to cope with severe deficiencies of relationships, including intense arguments or disagreement, and still show good intentions and faith, while hope that mutual understanding enhances gradually. Many of us might eventually understand that most relationship problems remain unresolved and we must somehow learn to live with them through wisdom and tolerance. Accordingly, the main questions are, 'Am I the type of person who can go through life in a conflict-laden environment and still make the best of it patiently? Why would I do that?' And then remember our answers forever whenever we face relationship conundrums.

Tolerance depends on personal virtues (or defects) reinforced by social norms and partners' level of expectations from their relationship. Most of us imagine that a perfect partner and ideal relationship are within our reach and a most natural expectation. We assume tolerance would hardly be required because we can find an ideal companion and atmosphere to nurture our personal needs. With such grand misperception, we do not learn that a marital relationship is built mainly around patience and evolves merely out of tolerance. Our parents and society do not teach us what tolerance means and requires. In fact, many recent social norms advocate low tolerance while pushing for independence and equality. We all think that *we deserve better*, and that there is something more interesting and less conflicting out there awaiting us as soon as we get out of our existing marital relationship.

Since partners cannot change themselves quickly and easily, their only hope should be to create an atmosphere where they can nurture an *enduring* level of faith and compassion. Tolerance is the foundation for building such an atmosphere, within which personality adjustments might be encouraged and nurtured. Tolerance means allowing our partner express and pursue his/her interests without our interference. Developing such atmosphere, perhaps as a last resort in some conflict-ridden cases, may in turn instigate the process of personal awareness and change. Simply, the idea is that, with tolerance, partners allow each other evolve as a person first (and then as a partner) in his/her own terms, until eventually (soon hopefully) they grasp each other's needs and ways.

On the other hand, tolerance does not mean accepting our partner's abuse or living with a selfish spouse in alienation and isolation. This attitude is more a sign of helplessness and desperation mixed with one's inability, or indecisiveness, to break away. Tolerance is unadvisable for extreme cases where partners are narcissistic or highly incompatible.

Acknowledging the peculiarities of our marital relationships and the inevitable impact of partners' psychological defects directly improves our tolerance level. It helps us realize why tolerance is a prerequisite of any marital relationship. In this sense, tolerance becomes an inherent product of our awareness. It grows rather automatically in line with the gradual growth of our wisdom. The reason this happens should be obvious: With awareness, our Ego subsides substantially and the decision about the level of tolerance is entrusted to Self. Self not only is more patient and passionate by its virtues, but also understands the helplessness and restrictions of our partner in handling his/her defects much better.

We can also understand why telling somebody to be more patient or tolerant cannot help him/her or the situation at all. Tolerance is mostly a function of self-confidence and learning how people's psychological defects control and render them helpless for the most part. Only then, we can increase our tolerance. As an example, at some stage in their relationship, a couple may realize that they always end up fighting when they have opposing views on a subject. They just cannot wait to prove their points and save their Egos at any cost. When partners learn how their Egos jump out to control those situations, and when they learn how useless winning or losing an argument is for saving their relationship, they become more tolerant of each other's disagreements even when they believe they are absolutely right about something. They just learn to let it go. Soon, both partners come to the same conclusion, if they are not too egoistical, and become less argumentative. Partners' awareness not only changes them directly, but also helps create an atmosphere to improve their attitudes and stop insisting on always being right. This would help them to not only calm down, but also realize the silliness and uselessness of their egoistic arguments.

i) Setting Our Tolerance Level

It is important to set a *level* for tolerance that is meaningful and reasonable according to our relationship's specific conditions. No scientific rule exists but, 1) we must never set the tolerance level (and apply it) during a relationship crisis. And, 2) we must remember that nowadays, couples usually have less tolerance than is normally justifiable and necessary for an average relationship. Our rising romanticism, strive for individualism and identity, and stress have made almost all of us less patient, and thus we begin our relationships with inadequate level of patience, tolerance, and compassion.

Nevertheless, we should have good criteria for *pre*setting a tolerance level that is logical and workable. It depends on the uniqueness of each relationship in terms of not only its atmosphere, but also partners' good intentions to improve their attitude and method of relating. We disallow daily turmoil, disagreements, and disappointments rule our mood and tolerance level. Instead, it is set only by reviewing the merits of our relationship objectively. We can adjust it occasionally whenever some major facts make it necessary to re-evaluate our marital situation.

Having an objective tolerance level helps in several ways. First, we become immune against Ego's interference during a crisis and forcing hasty or illogical decisions. Second, we maintain a rather high standard to measure the impact of any crisis against it and assess the health of our relationship. For example, we do not allow our spouse's fierce disagreement turn into an intolerable crisis when, for instance, the issue is whether s/he spends too much time with his/her friends. During such arguments, partners' Egos usually get too aroused and their tolerance level diminishes. Thus, the trick is to ensure that partners' brains do not rush in to reset the tolerance level during a few seconds (or days) of extreme rage. They must learn to make a judgment only after cooling down and reviewing the whole issue against their objective tolerance criterion.

Having a preset tolerance level means that we have taken our time, used our wisdom to assess our relationship rationally, and grasp its strengths and weaknesses. It also means that we always lean toward reconciliation, unless we have calmly and rationally arrived at the decision that we have *well* past the preset level of tolerance. As a simple approach, determining the level of tolerance is a matter of balancing the merits of our marital relationship against the conflicts and headaches it causes. Naturally, it is hard to measure and balance the evils and virtues of our relationships. Moreover, tolerance cannot be a matter of equilibrium between good and bad stuff in our relationship, but rather how much abuse we can take without hurting our health and stifling our soul.

ii) Misinterpreting Tolerance

Under some circumstances, our partner may misinterpret our tolerance as a sign of weakness and submission to his/her demands. Although this misunderstanding should not really affect our approach, we cannot allow it linger and dominate our relationship. If our partner misses or ignores our intention for saving our relationship, s/he would never appreciate our tolerance nor make any efforts of her/his own. At the same time, bragging about our tolerance usually causes a negative reaction, because it might sound we are doing our partner a big favour. That is actually exactly what we are doing, of course. We are doing ourselves, our partner, and our relationship a favour, but our partner would not appreciate our insinuation. Thus, we must make our tolerance known to our partner in a subtle way. (Gosh, how much work and diplomacy is needed nowadays just to maintain a basic relationship!)

As noted before, the purpose of tolerance is to create an atmosphere of cooperation for eventual change of attitudes and approach. If one partner is not involved in sustaining this environment, the efforts of the other partner would never help, other than increasing his/her own awareness and tolerance, of course. In addition, by not recognizing the purpose of our tolerance, our partner may in fact keep increasing his/her expectations and demands instead of adjusting them. Thus, while we are working hard to mitigate the sense of alienation, our partner may be completely off the track, pushing his/her own personal agenda, or maybe even testing our limits.

Thus, we must be firm in our communication and expressing our intentions of tolerance *tactfully*. Yet again, our hints should not sound like a threat or a sacrifice. Rather, we should portray our good intentions to make our relationship joyful for both of us, because we care about it. We do not only express our good intentions and tolerance, but also demonstrate them in our actions. We should be nice but show confidence, mainly by controlling our emotions, both positive and negative ones.

Tolerance and confidence are the prerequisites (and also the cause and effect) of each other. They reinforce each other within a person. As a confident person, we gain more tolerance against opposing views and arguments of our partner without feeling our Ego humiliated. And with tolerance we learn more about ourselves and our relationship in a rational way, and thus gain more control of our attitude and situation. The rational control of our emotions in our relationships directly enhances our confidence even further.

If our partner seems to be taking advantage of our tolerance, or continues with his/her misinterpretations of our intentions, we should rethink our options more carefully. We make a decision that serves us best personally, i.e., to accept the situation and tolerate some more or go for separation. If we choose the former option, we should create a personal approach and atmosphere for some kind of mutual understanding and communication, even if it is a rudimentary (passive) approach. We may even need to give in a little at the outset. If we can create an atmosphere to convey our initial thoughts to our partner, we might eventually succeed in discussing the concepts of alienation preparedness, tolerance, and cooperation for saving our relationship. If we conclude at the end that no such possibility exists, the only thing left to do is to project life under these substandard circumstances and the chance of a miracle turning things around. Then decide.

At the end, we are the one responsible for our tolerance level that makes sense to us. The whole idea of tolerance is for our benefit only, not our partner's. All our efforts are solely for increasing our objectivity, though our partner and our relationship benefit as well if the alienation process is slowed. In fact, the whole 'alienation preparedness' routine must be viewed as a personal attempt to learn about life and relationships without expecting any other rewards. Well, may be the only reward is facilitating our marital relationship and chances of enduring a life with a person who, in most cases, cannot think, feel, and act the same way we do.

Alienation Preparedness - Factor Four

Recognizing Our Opportunities and Fears

A big difference exists between tolerating out of fear or because of our confidence. We are acting from a position of confidence if we tolerate the harsh realities of our relationship according to the 'alienation preparedness' points noted here. We are monitoring and fighting the alienation process with a logical plan. We are confident that either the situation would improve eventually, or, when it deteriorates beyond our preset tolerance level, we know how to exit calmly without regrets for not having tried enough or separated sooner. On the other hand, if we tolerate out of fear of unknown future, a less desirable lifestyle, or whatever else, we are only delaying the act of separation while immersing deeper in the process of self-defeat and alienation. In this instance, we are not able to help ourselves, our partner, or our relationship in any way. The only way to help the situation and perhaps reverse the alienation process is to turn our fears into confidence. How we can achieve this, of course, depends on the nature of our fears and the strength of our personality.

People's various fears, insecurities, and vulnerabilities are too numerous and peculiar. We must list them out for ourselves as part of self-awareness. They affect our perceptions of life, decisions, and relationships. Yet, behind any fear, an opportunity awaits to be untapped. For example, behind the fear of separation (and loneliness) stands the great chance of finding 'who we are' away from our debilitating urge for a companion. Only we need personal courage to tap the opportunity that exists behind our fears. If we shake our minds only slightly to break out of normalcy and the freezing effect of our fears of change, most of us find a new world. We find courage to confront, and go beyond, the apparent limits within our crooked society and thus seize new opportunities. New life dimensions present themselves as we embrace the new opportunities. The joy of new discoveries and the relief from old fears would redefine our identity and create a refreshing sense of existence. Exploring every new opportunity also brings us a higher level of self-confidence. For example, we might have been tolerating our humiliating relationship out of fear of loneliness and inability to find another companion. Some of us in fact prefer an annoying partner to no partner, and we may have a good rationale behind it as well. However, behind those rationales could be our weak emotions, lack of confidence, self-pity, and other fears that turn into excuses and justifications. The truth is that without confidence we can neither be successful in our present (or future) relationship nor capture the essence of individualism. We also lose life's immense opportunities, including spirituality, that any intelligent person must explore on his/her own.

Our doubts about the viability of our relationships intensify our fears; not only the normal fears of loneliness and emotional breakdown, but also the fears of being wrong in our judgment about the state of our marriage and the possibility of reversing the alienation course. We doubt our partner ever understanding our needs and being able to provide the chance for a relatively peaceful companionship. We have doubts about the wisdom of staying in this convoluted marriage. We think that we should leave our partner before it is too late and before we lose our youth and attractiveness. These kinds of doubts and fears could deprive us from exploring the opportunity of making the relationship work in a more creative manner, confronting the alienation process head on, gaining self-awareness and tolerance, and possibly saving our marriage. We may suffer from our fears of either leaving our partner prematurely or staying too long in a marriage that might never work.

The bottom line is that we may conquer our doubts and fears only by building confidence and faith, and by redirecting our negative thoughts 180 degrees. With confidence, we give ourselves the opportunity that lies beyond our fears. We would surely do the right things when we measure our options from a platform of confidence, with some kind of faith in ourselves and our partner. We would do the right things when we confidently overcome the fears of doing the wrong things.

After living with a companion for a while, we learn to view life from only one dimension. We judge the value of our lives by the level of our success in maintaining a relationship. We ignore or undermine the value of an inherent relationship we (can) have with 'self.' With our fear of loneliness, we deprive ourselves of sensing and knowing our inner 'self' that can show us the main opportunities of life, starting with the recognition of our identity and deeper dimensions, including spirituality. We never realize and utilize our innate potentialities, which can provide us with the greatest secrets of our existence. If only we could bypass our fears of losing our existing spouse or never finding somebody else, we reach a new dimension of individualism that cannot be reached otherwise. This does not mean that we rush out to leave our spouse. Rather, we learn to face our relationships with confidence but total humility.

The bare minimal benefit of recognizing the inherent power and potentiality in our 'self' is the confidence we gain to repair our damaged relationship through tolerance and wisdom. On the other hand, we should beware of the high chance of growing a false confidence or overconfidence, which merely indicates our neglect to ponder the facts reiterated in this chapter adequately. Overconfidence shows low consciousness and hidden insecurities and leads to low tolerance. People's misperceptions about individualism and equality often give them a false sense of overconfidence, and thus a low tolerance level, while they become more arrogant every day. This misleading overconfidence destroys both chances of either having a good relationship or finding 'self.' It shows our immaturity and neediness. Conversely, real confidence makes a person humble within or without a relationship.

We are facing another dilemma of life: Our doubts and fears prevent us from boosting our confidence, and without confidence, we cannot conquer our fears and doubts. It is like the trite chicken and egg dilemma again—the old cliché. Most of us grow up with low self-image or often lose our self-confidence during life struggles. As a form of a psychological defect, with our compromised confidence we suffer from our fears and hurt our partner in so many ways, too, including our aggression and low tolerance. Thus, we must somehow gain our humble confidence to overcome our fears and also bring it to the rescue of our relationships. Initiating a self-awareness regimen is probably the best way to do that. We cannot buy or learn confidence easily even by taking confidence lessons and listening to expensive positive thinking lectures. Psychotherapy may help when pursued for a long period. On the other hand, humble confidence evolves automatically, though gradually, along with the rising level of our consciousness. This appears to be a much easier and cheaper alternative for gaining our confidence and all the good things that come along with it.

Alienation Preparedness - Factor Five

Admitting, Planning, and Playing Our Roles

To suppress the process of alienation, we must play an active role. We can just watch our relationship go sour, aggravate the situation by our retaliations or egoistic manoeuvres, or decide to play a positive role to prevent it from collapsing altogether. It does not matter, at this stage, if our partner does not understand how s/he is at least partly responsible for the problems. Because any effort centred on blaming or changing our partner's attitude would certainly fail. S/he would not even care to understand the scope of problems, while we most likely get trapped again in the same games of faultfinding, arguing and fighting, and challenging each other's Ego. Now, it is time to do something different if we really care. It is time to play a positive role.

The role we should play is different from everything we have been doing so far. The logic is simple and obvious. If we were doing the things right, we would not be in such a mess now anyway. Although we may think that it is our partner's faults that we cannot get along, we usually have doubts about this conclusion in our subconscious and conscience. Now, it does not really matter who is wrong or how much, anyway.

Those who have attributed all the problems to their partners are already divorced! They have somehow convinced themselves of their own perfection and never assumed that their Egos were responsible for at least some of the problems. They have already decided about the doomed prospect of their relationship and do not want to keep struggling and suffering anymore.

Often, however, most of us have doubts, because deep down we feel that perhaps some of our flaws inflame the fire of conflicts inadvertently. After all, we cannot be perfect, in spite of what our Ego keeps telling us non-stop. Another possibility for still being in a doomed relationship is that we have very low self-image and confidence. Alternatively, we might be still too optimistic naively about eventually forcing our partner to change. Anyway, we somehow entertain these possibilities and thus reinforce our doubts about the potential and viability of our relationships. In the final analysis, however, it does not matter which partner is mostly guilty if we are keen to correct the situation.

Then again, trying to play a new role, especially when we have already drifted a long way along the alienation path, is not an easy task all of a sudden. We may even feel embarrassed in front of our partner to suddenly appear much softer and more compromising than s/he ever thought we would (or could) be. The changes in us, if real, would definitely come across quite vividly, even though they may happen gradually. Our efforts to change our personal vision and approach to life (including marital life) would normally emerge slowly. However, our partner usually notices it at one instance when our attitude suddenly looks different in his/her eyes. We may have discussed our new ideas with our partner or not, but it is only his/her perceptions and our actual performance that s/he can believe, actually with some scepticism at the beginning. Nevertheless, our new role in defusing the process of alienation grows along with our understanding of our true 'self.' Accordingly, it is not too difficult to stay humble and play our marriage-saviour role. However, we should be cautious about the way we approach this sensitive matter, because we are a novice, and because our doubts and fears still linger in our subconscious and make us look hesitant and vulnerable.

Initially, we may depend on our Model to play the new role, while we become completely convinced of the merits of our new mission and become committed to it. Model can be instrumental in containing our Ego until we learn to draw upon our Self for facing our partner's persistence to make us fail. S/he would possibly be resentful of our calmer approach to solving problems and ignoring many topics that usually cause arguments and faultfinding urges. S/he would eventually get used to the new person we have become and most likely appreciate the change too. Then s/he may join in with us to make things better, though perhaps not initially, because of her/his doubts and suspicions as to what we are up to now.

Therefore, understanding our new role and playing it properly is a major step for slowing down and defusing the alienation process. We accept this challenging responsibility only with the aim of helping ourselves, and perhaps our relationship eventually. The most important role we must play consists of those steps enumerated about acknowledging relationship needs and personal flaws—Alienation Preparedness Factors One and Two. We must learn about ourselves and relationships, set our tolerance level, and all the rest of it just to make sure we have played an active role in shaping our approach and thoughts for running a workable relationship—maybe even finding a more appropriate relationship model. We want to be certain that when we surrender on the alienation road, or opt for eventual separation, we have extended our utmost efforts to avoid it (considering our own defects). We want to wait until there is no chance of communicating and understanding, although we have set our Ego aside and dealt with our relationship only through Self. We understand the need to build our confidence and tolerance with commitment and persistence, until 'alienation preparedness' possibly succeed. Taking all these initiatives is hard. However, showing initiative is the main idea behind tolerance. Through tolerance, we should *learn* to give up our egoism and make a good use of our Self. We want to play our role effectively.

We admit the complexity of people's psychological defects, which play a major role in causing marital problems. We acknowledge that we all have extreme difficulty in realizing and defeating our idiosyncrasies. We admit that tolerance is an absolute requirement of living with another individual. However, we also set a rational level for it based on the characteristics of our relationship and our partner's depth of defects. We understand that we are attempting to make changes in our approach and attitude by being an active agent of change, but more importantly by being a true example of change. And, of course, we should understand that most likely we would fail despite our sincere efforts to implement substantive changes. We admit that the alienation process may continue to deteriorate beyond repair despite our good intentions and struggles. We know that our only reward is to bring our marital relationship to a tolerable level, if possible, as a last resort. The goal is to gain back our relative independence (in and out of our relationship) without having any regrets later on. We want to be sure we have made our best and honest efforts to correct the mess that marriage partners usually create for each other.

Once we understand all these facts about our role and their wide implications, we set out to implement our thoughts. We plan about discussing some of the issues with our partner, how, and when. We plan about the areas of personal defects that require more care, awareness, and improvement. We plan about the needed changes that we must pursue actively, personally and perhaps with our partner's help later. We plan our steps, measure our progress, learn from our mistakes, and hope for the best. If necessary, we might revise our plans later and devise more challenging and detailed ones along with our newer refine thoughts.

Playing our role diligently and patiently with compassion would be tricky and important. Especially, if we are reaching the end of the alienation road, we keep in mind that this is our last chance and the right time to **think of marriage now that it appears like the time of divorce**.

Alienation Preparedness - Factor Six

Making an Objective Judgment and Decision

To live or leave: That is the doubt!

Usually, the most annoying problem in a marital relationship is our 'doubt' about its quality and viability. Should we continue to *live* with our inconsiderate partner, or time has come to *leave* him/her? This doubt persists even when we have set proper tolerance criteria and follow the alienation preparedness routine discussed in this chapter.

We suffer needlessly when problems (and doubts) remain unsettled in our minds. We recognize this basic dilemma and tolerate it consciously or subliminally as a necessity for social adaptation. Yet, we also believe that every problem needs a resolution. If we cannot get rid of the problems, we must at least come to terms with them. In fact, it is often more practical, and even more effective in the long run, to come to terms with problems rather than solving them or destroying their source—which often appears to be our partner. We try to see a problem as an inevitable fact in modern societies when it is not possible to eliminate it. For example, if we learn to accept marital problems as a social pandemic, we may be able to take relationship pains less personal. We might learn to cope with them in a rather passive 'relationship model' perhaps, hoping to create a tolerable relationship despite its irresolvable problems. The purpose of a good judgment and decision is to settle our marital problems in our minds, especially when they cannot be solved. Ignoring marital problems—on an alienation course toward divorce—appears the fastest and simplest way out. It is a solution, but it is neither a creative one nor an effective way of viewing and settling a problem.

Often problems have no solution, nor can we come to terms with them—like our deteriorating socioeconomic condition, or a wicked, nagging spouse. A major problem may break a person to the verge of committing suicide as the only option for coming to terms with the problem. Or, a terminally ill person may prefer a decent, quick exit to avoid pain and degradation. At the other extreme, smaller problems that remain undetected might persistently cause suffering and stress. We must look deep down in our psyche to find the reasons, and their legitimacy, for our lacklustre life and failing relationships. At least we might understand the scope of our problems, which may be major or minor. Conversely, we may feel that we have problems, but cannot identify their causes on our own.

Another quandary is that no reliable criteria exist nowadays for measuring the degree of our marital problems. We wonder whether our problems are real or imaginary, major or minor, in comparison to a typical marital relationship in our mishmash culture. Of course, we may explain our problems in general terms, such as the lack of communication or understanding, but these typical diagnoses cannot help us see the roots of our problems. We can seek professional help and marriage counselling, but at the end, we cannot quite locate and feel our problems unless we make a point of measuring and judging them through self-assessment. We must take on the responsibility of defusing the alienation process in hopes of resolving the problems eventually and salvaging our marriage. Otherwise, the most reasonable solution would be to end the doomed relationship as soon as possible.

Partners could drag a dead relationships on their backs until death do them part. However, a relationship contaminated with irresolvable problems would only cause more sufferings, and may restrict access to opportunities outside their relationship. We know these facts when we face our doubt about an unsettling marital situation. However, before pronouncing our relationships dead, we wish to examine them for any vital sign to ensure there is no chance of revival.

To make a judgment of any value, especially for such a crucial decision, we should obviously step outside our Ego barrier. After all, our impartial judgment about marital problems is ONLY for our own benefit, and thus we ought to become more altruistic and realistic about the level of personal egoism we can allow for such a serious judgment.

Being a good judge of our relationships is not easy, of course. Impartiality is impossible when our Ego is the judge, which is often the case. Ego has become the nucleus of our individuality and identity and the dominant force in our relationships. It has overtaken most of us to the extremes of perceiving and assessing the world and events only from Ego's point of view. Still we let it judge and decide for us. In this tainted environment, it would be extremely hard (but wise) to delve into our true 'self' even partially to mitigate our prejudices and biases.

On the other hand, always some obstacles hinder our objective judgment about the state and content of our marriage. For one thing, the information always appears incomplete, which raises our doubts about our partner's intentions and the sources of problems. Sometimes, we want to give our partner the benefit of our doubts, especially if we become partially aware of our own flaws, prejudices, and biases. And sometimes we remain optimistic about our partner eventually smartening up and changing his/her attitude and approach.

These erratic perceptions merely increase our doubts and delay our decision, which we must eventually make.

Alienation preparedness is for helping us mitigate our doubts as well as our prejudices by utilizing our newly earned awareness and wisdom. During this process, we accumulate all the relevant information, including the intensity of partners' flaws and the depth of their good intentions. Then we set our tolerance criteria and level. We understand and acknowledge our fears and opportunities, and we play our reconciliatory role actively. If we take all these steps properly and faithfully, our judgment is bound to be more rational and impartial.

Without alienation preparedness, we cannot make a conscious judgment about the state of our relationship and thus have difficulty making rational decisions. We remain doubtful about many variables in our relationship and our options, until our partner forces a decision upon us, or we make a hasty and irrational decision in a moment of distress and Ego attack. Naturally, these are exactly the kind of decisions that are disastrous and we would like to avoid.

The Awareness Puzzle

Awareness is mostly for grasping the underlying problems of our relationship without getting into deep analysis and drawing conclusions right away. We are simply looking for clues and signs of problems to draw a general picture about our relationship. This fact-finding process demands total objectivity. It requires staying clear from criticism and fast conclusions. When we first look for relationship problems, we are not compelled to acquire our partner's participation or consent. We do not have to ask our partner to sit with us, argue, blame each other, get our Egos worked up, and at the end get nothing accomplished. Rather, problem diagnosis is merely a personal awareness exercise. We do everything, at least initially, by ourselves, without the involvement of our partner. For example, if we have lost our interest or love for our partner, we should admit it honestly, instead of looking for excuses as to 'Why I have lost my love or respect for him/her.' The reasons are only important at the next stage, only if the possibility of regaining our love and respect for him/her exists. We do not even have to admit our faults to our partner if we do not want to, but at least we should become aware of our own erratic emotions, and eventually start working on them.

We may think that we are aware of all the factors contributing to alienation and we are aware of the process and the rest of it. Yet, it is often merely our superficiality about the meaning of awareness that makes us flop. In addition, we often *think* that we are aware and proactive in strengthening our marital relationship, but our partner's lack of awareness and faults cause the problems anyway. We may even believe that our awareness efforts and practicing certain roles to prevent alienation are simply a waste of our time, or at least not fair, because we are doing all the work and showing interest to save our marriage while our partner appears more careless every day.

While we can aim for the awareness of both partners and their influence on each other to strengthen the development of an alienation preparedness routine, we can only be in control of our own awareness process and progress. We are responsible for playing our role consciously without being disturbed or discouraged by our partner's apathy. Our awareness means that we accept our partner's resistance and deal with the possibility of negative attitude and psychological defects of our partner, which may directly interfere and hinder our attempts to spawn awareness in our marital relationship. We must keep playing our role.

One essential fact to remember is that, in most cases, we end up following the alienation preparedness process on our own. Like all other types of awareness and enlightenment experiences, marital awareness is also a personal objective we pursue for our benefit. It would prove to be a useful way of calming ourselves and reducing the stress caused by the unknown sources of marital conflicts and quarrels. More importantly, however, marital awareness is a personal endeavour, because, in the final analysis, the information and wisdom we gain through awareness can help us make an objective decision about our relationship and future. We cooperate with our partner and show interest in pursuing a joint awareness process as much and long as possible, but then we would be responsible for our decision, especially if it must be 'separation.'

When we speak to our partner from an awareness platform, it does not necessarily mean that s/he understands or agrees with our views and approach for solving our problems. We need to establish common grounds upon which awareness oriented communication can emerge. However, we must first work on a preliminary self-awareness for ourselves. Often we think we are aware of the situation and problems when in fact we are only focusing on our partner's faults and blaming him/her for everything. In such cases, our awareness is not real and objective, but rather a faultfinding endeavour. Our persistence to convince our partner about relationship problems, and that s/he is in fault, merely shows our egoistic mentality. However, unfortunately, this is the most common approach that partners pursue naively. Focusing on our partner's faults and flaws is usually the easiest way of copping out, instead of learning to cope with relationships' sad realities in the new era through self-awareness. We refuse to understand our responsibility in causing conflicts and our role for pursuing an alienation preparedness regimen.

As a productive option, we should develop a high level of awareness slowly by activating Self and becoming a selfless and compassionate person. We must set aside our judgment of our partner's faults and instead focus on the alienation process and our role for preventing our marriage breakdown, if possible. We do not want to apply awareness as another level of

scrutiny on our partner's lack of understanding and cooperation. Instead, we turn inwardly to find our own faults that contribute to alienation, and only then find those conditions of our
relationship that make us incompatible or unable to communicate. Otherwise, we would not attain the meaning and purpose
of awareness. we would only keep blaming our partner forever
and dissolve further in our egoistic personality. Our crooked
approach to awareness would only create more alienation and
friction than help. Naturally, under these circumstances, we
also get frustrated and give up quickly when we encounter our
partner's retaliatory actions and spite. Our insincerity and egoism would only confuse us and alienate our partner further too.

The bottom line is that we pursue an awareness exercise
because we sincerely care about our relationship as well as our
life. That is a significant motive and target. The goal is to help
ourselves by remaining objective to identify the real problems
and set the course of our lives in a proper direction. We should
admit that awareness is more about finding our own faults and
share of misunderstandings. It is more a process of bringing
our Ego in check. And it is more a search for means of enhancing our communication with our partner. Only as a sec-
ondary objective, we try to find other sources and external factors that also contribute to alienation. At this stage, we only try
to learn about (become aware of) the roots of problems. To the
extent we can work on the problems unilaterally, we may initiate plans and programs to improve our attitude and approach.
To the extent that we need to change other things, including
our partner's attitude or perceptions at least, we cannot demand them quickly without first establishing a mutual understanding and drawing a sensible plan.

Thinking Romance and Remarriage

When the thoughts of separation and divorce overwhelm us, it
is the best opportunity to awaken our mood of romanticism to

put off spite and urges of retaliation that are boiling inside us. This is a difficult task—and perhaps even suggesting it appears pure silly—when partners are on the verge of breakdown psychologically and emotionally. Yet, the main purpose of self-awareness is to learn control our Ego and then notice our emotions beginning to adjust automatically. The question is, 'How to watch our Ego and curb it in such trying circumstances?' One way is to think of our marriage ended and our partner not being around to cause frictions and hurts. Creating this image in our heads realistically would feel impossible initially, because of the tension of disagreements and the intensity of abuse we feel our partner has inflicted upon us. Actually, we probably want our partner dead or at least out of our life immediately, instead of cherishing him/her again like good old days. However, with *alienation preparedness mentality*, we may eventually cool down and redirect the energy wasted negatively on hostility to positively charged awareness. All these efforts would be successful, of course, only if there is still respect and some sense of attraction between partners.

At this point, *thinking marriage* is the last resort for married couples before actually going through with the separation option. By thinking marriage, partners assume that their present marriage has ended and they are now facing one last chance to enter into a new marriage contract. Except that now partners are wiser, have better knowledge of each other, and do not think that writing a contract would be unromantic. This is obviously possible only if both partners are willing to reduce their expectations and choose a relationship model that gives partners a higher level of independence while observing the sanctity of their marriage. Nonetheless, at this stage, we do not care anymore whether it is romantic to sign a contract or not. Rather, the whole point is to clarify the practicality of both partners' lowering their expectations from their relationship. We would like to assess the possibility of renegotiating a contract with our partner in which we can identify our needs, as well as our commitments, before we agree to re-enter into a new marital relationship.

To overcome our anger and maybe rekindle some romantic moods, we can think of funny experiences and delightful memories that we have shared, including the birth of our children. Instead of feeling pity for ourselves and our wasted lives, we can try to elevate some sense of compassion by recalling our partner's devotions, triumphs, and hopes. We can try to generate some creative thoughts about the good aspects of our relationship (past and present) to find out how inadvertently we have let our oversensitivity and personal quirks ruin everything. Nobody is to be blamed because this is not the right time for it, and there is not even time for it. Now, it is time to revive the moods of romanticism, if possible, to stir up some positive energy during this time of crisis. We must somehow reconcile our differences before falling into despair and a self-destructive state of mind. To be honest, if no romance is left between partners, very little chance of reconciliation exists, considering the intensity of problems that have carried partners to this level of animosity. Realistically, in spite of attraction and romance, we may eventually feel tired of struggling to save our marriage so many times and failing repeatedly; so it would seem quite logical to quit.

Romanticism for our purpose at this sad and controversial stage of a relationship implies mostly compassion than passion. The mere act of stopping our reactionary and retaliatory attitude can reflect our compassion, which is the basic means of romanticism. It is not even necessary to be expressed or played together with our partner either, but mostly felt individually. One way is to recall (maybe even sarcastically) the romantic memories of yesteryears and then perhaps use our Model later to share them with our partner even if it might sound rather foolish under the circumstance. The basic idea is to get rid of negative moods and thoughts, at least for a while. Later, when the situation seems more stable, we may add some additional flavour to this simple 'first step' by gradually approaching our partner with love, awareness, and eventually some novel plans to build a new joint life.

If we cannot overcome our negative feelings of ongoing disappointments with our partner, in spite of our efforts to remain compassionate and show understanding, then we have possibly reached the last stage.

Reviving the moods of romanticism in a broken marriage seems impractical and futile. Yet, this suggestion is based on the author's own personal experiences and positive results— although a divorce became inevitable ten years later anyway. From a logical perspective, we can note that, in the absence of any other option but divorce, following an unorthodox approach of feeling and expressing romance is our last resort to turn things around, so that partners may hopefully cool down and make a valid judgment. Unfortunately, during these trying times, when marital conflicts feel overwhelming, we usually adopt a hostile and controversial approach, which often only expand hatred and expedite separation foolishly. Only retaliation seems to make us feel good! But we are wrong. It is easy to be a spiteful person. But the art of living is to finally grasp our sense of selflessness, which automatically revives all the romantic instances of our lives, too, including the ones with our inconsiderate, foolish spouse. It is not hard to change gear and reach for the more tranquilizing emotions of forgiveness and love, if only we can overcome our false pride, and disengage our Ego. We can activate our Model to express our raw emotions, if we have a hard time using Self in showing our very deep feelings. Sometimes, we can make a good use of our Model, and this could be one of those occasions.

My personal experience relates to the first occasion when my wife and I decided to separate—about fifteen years ago. Despite our heated power struggles and confrontations, we agreed to see a marriage counsellor on the recommendation of our family physician (after giving us enough stress medications). The counsellor had an impressive background, with a Ph.D. in psychology and many years of experience in marriage counselling. We visited him every week for about three months and explained our backgrounds, concerns, and our relationship situation. He gave us his professional advice, and we covered many grounds throughout this exploratory and reconciliatory process. At the end, he bluntly announced that he did not think we had a chance. I remember that day very well. We left his office in silence and delved into our own thoughts and emotions. We felt that we were really on our own and nobody could help us, perhaps as a fair judge, for pinpointing the problems that the marriage counsellor had not been able to rectify.

It became clear to me, at the end, that it did not matter what the sources of problems were anyway. We are humans, after all, and full of flaws and foolishness. So many things entered my mind, and finally I realized that I had to change my approach, if only because that was our only hope. We were getting ready for divorce anyway, so why not give ourselves a last chance by thinking marriage in these dying moments of our relationship.

Gradually, I discovered many things through deeper self-awareness and reading related books. I learned a great deal about marriage and divorce. I did not submit to whims and ways of my wife, nor did she to mine. Rather, we made a point to express an explicit form of compassion, friendship, and occasional feelings of romanticism. In particular, enhancing the moods of romanticism was not easy for either of us, because of our recent negative experiences and our inherently logical (less emotional) minds. In many instances, we drew on our Model to make romantic gestures, which although did not appear as sincere as we liked them to be, they still made a positive impact on our relationship.

With a very rudimentary alienation preparedness process that my wife and I built gradually, we were successful in re-

versing the progress of alienation and accomplished the task
that even a specialist assumed impossible. We achieved this
only by faith and resorting to a more suitable relationship
model for us—at least the one I thought might work. I cannot
say whether we both came to the same conclusions simultaneously or not. But my guess is that one of us played a more active role in propagating the alienation preparedness process
without perhaps even recognizing what s/he was about to do
or achieve. And, of course, both of us quickly encouraged, or
at least agreed with, the intentions of the other one. Our relationship was not perfect by a long shot at this time yet. However, it had improved a lot, from retaliation and spite to a more
civilized and romantic approach based on tolerance, accepting
the fact that personal defects cannot be defused quickly, avoiding hasty invalid judgments, giving each other more independence, separating our financial affairs, and resisting futile
egoistic arguments.

Ten years later, we made another valid judgment and decided that it was time to quit, and we did. The main question
and doubt in my mind is whether we should have separated in
the first place ten years earlier. Maybe one or both of us now
regret our decision to reconcile, but then (fifteen years ago) we
had decided that giving ourselves another chance was a wiser
decision. The problem with life nowadays is that most of our
important decisions do not prove totally satisfactory or effective at the end, for bringing us a relative sense of happiness, or
for helping us resolve some of our fundamental doubts about
living. No real solutions seem to exist anyway for many of our
primary problems! That is life!

Life's major decisions, including marriage and divorce, are
irreversible, too. Therefore, our life experiences related to
these decisions can hardly help us. Such is life!

PART III

Hardships

CHAPTER EIGHT
Marriage Conundrums

THE vast amounts of partners' idiosyncrasies make couples incompatible and impose major marital problems. These common conundrums are complex already, but often some unique circumstances evolve in most relationships too. Thus, studying the health of any particular relationship becomes difficult. It gets tricky and sticky to grasp the depth of issues and find solutions. On top of that, partners are usually too stubborn, dogmatic, and spiteful. These common flaws make couples incapable of agreeing on the main causes of their conflicts or possible solutions offered. Many books about marriage conundrums have provided insightful hints and recommendations for decades with no tangible results. Marriages are actually getting more unreliable and sadder every day, because we do not know anything about relationship needs and the right factors for partners' compatibility in the first place—when couples still have a chance to make a rational decision. Some irrelevant factors, including love and loneliness, often make us jump into a marriage and then suffer its repercussions for years or decades. The irony is that many simple issues cause major hardships in relationships merely due to partners' naiveté and impatience. Some of these basic causes of relationship hardships are discussed in this chapter.

Communication Hurdles

Communication breakdown is one major cause of marital conflicts. While couples seem to understand the content and
method of their partner's communication quite well before
marriage, they usually have great difficulty communicating
after marriage. It is safe to assume that if communication was
lacking or felt problematic, partners would have wisely not
married. If this is true, then something goes terribly wrong
after the marriage. Some of the possibilities are as follows:

- While partners may have assumed that they had good (or at
  least bearable) communication before marriage, they really
  did not know what communication consists of, and what it
  is supposed to achieve.
- We all have a tendency to think positively before marriage
  about the way we know our partners and how clearly we
  understand the contents and means of our communication.
  Then we are shocked more every day after marriage when
  we realize our naive initial optimism. We realize not only
  our erroneous assumptions about understanding our partner's expectations, but also the way we grasp each other's
  simple words, thoughts, and method of communication.
  Communication breakdown is mostly because we do not
  grasp, or misinterpret, each other's intentions and needs.
- The level of listening, giving and forgiving, which are all
  parts of communication, diminishes because partners' initial
  intentions of impressing (and perhaps manipulating) each
  other subside after marriage.
- The level of partners' sensitivity toward each other's feelings
  somehow diminishes, most likely inadvertently. While
  premarital communication seems to be tailored for luring
  our partners, post-marital communication is more focused
  on domination of the situation and our partners.

- At the same time, partners become oversensitive and impatient about the way their partner treats them.
- Partners refocus on other issues of life, which appear to be more pressing, and thus find less time, and need to spend on proper communication. It appears that partners do not pay enough attention to each other's needs and words, even though they may continue to be mentally and physically attracted to each other.
- On many occasions, the level of respect declines because partners find out more about each other's vulnerabilities. The idol they had envisioned in a partner proves to be quite defective. The contents, means, and level of communication are, of course, a function of respect.
- Partners often overestimate their tolerance level and put a great level of faith in the power of their love.
- Partners assume they know about relationships' unique needs, but almost nobody knows about the real purposes and complexities of relationships in the new era. Thus, their communication channels collapse, while other irresolvable relationship deficiencies press and demand some form of cooperation and understanding.
- Partners face family or personal issues and they cannot see things the same way, or they are not prepared to accept each other's conclusions and solutions, merely out of spite or perhaps with good personal reasons. Differences of opinions and value systems make communication incoherent and unproductive.

When communication hurdles emerge and we are unable to improve the process, it becomes increasingly impossible to bring it back under control. Some basic communication issues grow into major relationship obstacles where no single problem can be discussed and resolved. It appears as if all other aspects of the relationship have stopped functioning as well. The moods and feelings change and partners start to be suspicious of each other. We stop expressing our needs to our partner since we find it a waste of time, because not only s/he is not listening, but also we do not understand the content of our communication. The things we say to each other do not make sense and they are contrary to everything we thought we had agreed on implicitly and perhaps even explicitly in our earlier communications.

We can analyse the contents of communication to find out the causes of frictions or the lack of interest to discuss seemingly contentious issues. We can also observe how personal insecurity and unsatisfied needs of partners always interfere and override the context of the intended communication. In many cases, communication is convoluted by the hidden personal agendas, fears, insecurities, and other psychological defects that are not obvious or admitted to by partners. Under these circumstances, it does not matter what we talk about and what the contents of communication are. We always revert to the same crooked personal perceptions and draw on our inherent idiosyncrasies to express our anger and blame our partners for everything. Any topic of conversation becomes only a prelude to raise the same old grievances. The blames may be well founded or a product of hasty retaliations. Nevertheless, the results are the same as far as communication ineffectiveness is concerned. Unless these underlying problems are resolved, the contents of communication would not be of any relevance in harmonizing the process and results.

The method of communication also influences partners' reaction quite drastically. For example, showing interest, concern, and compassion instils a favourable atmosphere for dialogue, and enhances partners' trust in each other as well as their personal confidence. Of course, this approach works as long as partners appreciate each other's concerns and respect the rules of a good communication process. Acknowledging the conflicts and our partner's feelings usually helps the process. However, on some occasions, one partner keeps increasing his/her demands in spite of all the compassion that s/he receives from his/her partner—a symptom of severe psychological shortfalls that block the improvement of communication process permanently.

A similar communication hurdle emerges when we think we are giving more to our partner than s/he is ever able to understand and repay. We believe we are more attentive to his/her needs, show more concern and compassion, and thus feel deprived of receiving equivalent attention and appreciation. In fact, we are baffled by our partner's rising demands despite everything we do for him/her already. This feeling of non-equilibrium in the amount of affection and care by one partner always emerges in the tone and texture of communication and results in chaotic exchanges of charged feelings instead of a dialogue.

The problem of inadequate affection and understanding in family relationships is recognized widely. The major remedy prescribed by many books is that partners should become more conscious and show extra affection. This suggestion means that we must make even more use of our Model to produce and present more affection beyond what we naturally feel. We sense a pressure to play an unnatural role, to show extra affection even when we do not feel affectionate for so many reasons. It is necessary and nice that partners understand each other's problems and show empathy. However, in reality, most of us cannot resolve our psychological shortfalls by a mere exchange of affection. One partner's unconditioned and superficial show of affection only boosts other partner's Ego and leads to more demands for recognition and attention. This feels and appears like rewarding our partner's unjustifiable demands and manipulations. This may continue to the point of complete submission of one partner and domination by the other.

In addition, for some of us, the use of Model, above what we can naturally handle and believe in, feels untrue and torturous. We eventually drop the act or show our discomfort indirectly in some other ways in our subsequent communications. The major problem is that, even with extra affection, the communication deficiencies would most likely never get resolved. For example, when the sources of problems relate to partners' personalities, never-ending selfish needs, or psychological defects (e.g., Ego, insecurity, fear), extra affection cannot remedy any of these problems in the long run. Despite some temporary improvements, the original unrest, demands, suspicions, and all other flaws in partners' personalities resurface. In some cases, actually extra affection would hurt a chance for logical communication.

When our customary communication *methods* cause confrontation, partners feel the chaos and disappointments. The Egos of both parties get hurt and agitated as soon as the communication begins, because they anticipate the regular abuse and arguments. The atmosphere creates hurdles and resistance to tackle the *contents* of the communication, because the method is not reliable and trusted. For example, (A) starts to talk about something and then (B) interrupts inadvertently and makes a hasty comment or correction, which is unrelated to the main content of (A)'s communication. (A) becomes upset and tries to correct (B) for unsolicited and irrelevant comment and then their intense arguments prevent them to really attend to the substantive and pressing matters of their married life. For instance, they agree to talk about budget and financial plans for the upcoming year. (B), who may be struck by a recent thought or stress, reminisces some of his/her past hurts. S/he uses the occasion to relieve the frustrations of let us say (A)'s carelessness and lack of passion, *or perhaps about not having enough shoes!* S/he hastily expresses his/her dissatisfaction with (A) being secretive, perhaps about the amount of money s/he makes. When (A) shockingly asks for an explanation, (B) replies, "Because you have kept your bank account activities secret." Most likely other reasons are behind this outburst, but it reflects the general mistrust between them. Most importantly, however, the main intention of reviewing the budget is ignored completely.

Thus, the disagreement over an unrelated point prevents partners to continue with their initial intentions and contents of communication. Sometimes a partner may realize his/her destructive interjection and/or a mistake in expressing an opinion. Yet, s/he does not want to change his/her position because of false pride, or just to prove s/he never makes a mistake. S/he does not want to leave a precedent for being wrong even once.

A lack of communication often reflects partners' fear and anticipation of clashes anytime they try to communicate with each other. This is the result of many years of negative experiences, and partners' reactionary and defensive attitude toward all communications between them. Most often, compulsive reaction and anger disrupt the whole process before partners even get a chance to discuss the main contents of the communication.

When communication is tense, both partners only push their ideas and Egos without any attention to communication contents and other person's intentions. Soon, they would be arguing about irrelevant issues only for blaming each other and making noise. In these situations, a possible solution is to enforce a one-way communication method for a while. In this method, (A) explains his/her points, *about only one selected topic,* while (B) only listens and makes notes. Partner (B) should leave the meeting with an understanding of (A)'s concerns and then spend sometime to reflect on them. If (B) is genuinely interested in improving their communication, s/he can make real efforts to see (A)'s viewpoints without becoming too defensive and upset. When (B) is ready to go back in a few days with answers and suggestions, this time only (B) speaks and (A) listens without interfering or making gestures to provoke unrest and anger. (A) would have his/her chance in a few days again to reflect on (B)'s comments and ideas. This process continues until one topic is relatively resolved. And then to the next item on the agenda, which is prepared by both partners' contributions and inputs. In this process, partners use their negotiating skills, *to solve one issue at a time,* except that they do not talk simultaneously and spontaneously before having the chance to contemplate their partner's problems and proposed suggestions.

One-way communication is a lengthy and stressful process for both partners, especially the partner whose turn is to only listen. The idea of restraining our rage and egoism for a day or two to only contemplate on our partner's words is torturous. However, for couples with communication issues, but genuine interest to improve the situation, one-way-a-time communication method often helps. This method stresses on the control of anger and focuses on communication contents, instead of jumping from issue to issue and losing track of the intentions of the communication. The ideal would be to have a third person mediate and moderate the process at least until partners learn to follow the rules of communication and control their reactionary attitude and anger.

Withdrawal and avoiding dialogue to prevent confrontations may seem the only option to us to reduce our relationship hardships somewhat. In fact, it may prove to be the case at the end other than separation. First, we should try, however, to keep communication channels open as long as possible. If a two-way (simultaneous) communication method does not work, we can resort to the rotating one-way method and extend genuine efforts to learn to communicate, because without it any marriage is doomed. That is a kind of hardship we must accept in order to deter the chances of bigger agonies.

Expecting Our Partner to Change

Expecting our partner to change is another common source of conflict and agony in relationships. When we are young and naïve, we consider our partner's declaration of love a kind of submission to (or at least acceptance of) our way of thinking and living. Immediately, we assume that not only we understand each other, but also love would motivate our partner become the image we have of a perfect spouse. Thus, we get married. Initially, we expect our partner to guess and understand our thoughts and needs and adjust her/himself accordingly. We expect change in all levels and all matters. We want change of attitude, thoughts, beliefs, way of dressing, etiquettes, relationships and friends, eating habits, things we like or dislike around the house, the way and time we choose to do things, philosophy and outlook on life, political views, tastes in things, on and on we can go. When this does not happen automatically on the power of our love per se, we eventually lose our patience and directly ask for changes that we believe are overdue. And, again, when we do not see true changes, we get frustrated and angry with our partner for being so stubborn and not willing to cooperate (change). We demand change or try to manipulate our partner to get the results we need and reduce our hardships.

In all, our first mistake is to assume that the strength of our love would overcome our partner's natural resistance to change. Our second mistake is our assumption that s/he can change and is deliberately resisting it. Mostly the appearance of resistance and carelessness toward our requests and expectations agitates and frustrates us. Thus, we continue to get into arguments and fights. Naturally, we blame our partner for being the cause of these arguments, especially for refusing to admit his/her stubbornness amidst many other faults.

The fact is that people hardly change, since their personalities are shaped mostly by their unconscious urges, which drive them to be who they are. They cannot even control their think-ing and attitudes, which are driven by their conscious and sub-conscious minds most often. Only for social adaptation and acceptance purposes, sometimes we can draw upon our Model to portray an attitude of change. However, this tentative change fails to stabilize and we revert to our original form soon, as change is not internalized and we cannot subdue our old habits and needs. Permanent and stable changes are in-duced by some major psychological motivation or personal convictions through experience and enlightenment. We do not change because others ask us to, and not even because we want to, but only because our mental capabilities have reached the level in which real 'change' brings the truth we trust.

Our unrealistic assumptions and expectations about 'changing our partner' lay the foundation for many marital conflicts and agonies. If we recognize that change is not auto-matic and controllable at the level we desire, then we can be-come a little more understanding and flexible with our partner on this matter. We must not only evaluate our intentions for expecting our partner to change, but also remember that they cannot do it readily even when they work on it very hard. We may then stop attributing our partner's lack of change to spite or his/her purposeful resistance. Of course, some kinds of per-sonality changes may be possible, even at some noticeable degrees, when a person keeps his/her Model at full alert to play certain expected roles. However, these changes are most likely superficial, and the degree of change is not fundamental. Overall, personal changes are simply unattainable without a full intention and a long process of self-awareness.

Why Do We Expect Change?

We want our partner to change for many reasons. For one thing, we desire a routine that is most convenient for us, or because our partner's habits, values, or ethics irritate us. Another reason is our strong tendency to dominate others and make them do things our ways. Most of us have strong inner urges to control events and others. We must dominate others or else feel dominated and overruled. We attempt to change our partners' personality to make them more subservient, dependent, and agreeable to our frame of mind. We imagine that we can save our marriage only by making our partner change so that the situation does not get out of hand. Still another prominent reason for demanding change is our 'need for feeling loved and testing our partner's devotion.' It satisfies our urge for possession too. Our partner's dependence on us (for love) gives us a sense of security (because we feel wanted, needed, or a sense of being in control of our marriage). We want to be *spoiled* to curb our insecurities.

We also demand change obsessively only to satiate our need for ELove. When our partner refuses to change, our Ego is threatened and our need for being loved feels under attack. All along, we believe we are honest and true in terms of our love for our partner, while s/he seems more careless every day. 'Love' and 'being in need of love' are different, though. While 'love' is a mythical expression of beauty, devotion, giving, and forgiving, 'being in need for love' reflects our selfishness, demanding attitude, and the overall dependency urge of humans. We think love, but in fact are influenced and driven by our selfish 'need for being loved'—to be spoiled, as a new fad in relationships.

Thus, we take our partner's inability to change as a sign of not only his/her vindictive persistence to contradict us, but also not loving us anymore. We always believe that s/he resists change only because s/he does not care about us enough, and not that s/he cannot change. Love and need for love are good topics for understanding the self, ego, and model aspects of our personality. Even when we attempt to invoke our Self and inherent spiritual need for love, often Ego interferes with its 'need for love.' All the expressions and pretences of love are reflections of Model manifesting the feeling of love without really understanding the true implications of selfless love. Clearly, all three aspects of personality reflect some type of love when we express or demand it, but it is mostly Ego driven.

Sometimes, we may try to change to make our partner happy or show that we care. Therefore, we activate our Model to portray the change. We force ourselves to make the best use of our Model to display a change of attitude. We do it for a while, but most likely fail to bring about a real change. Model is the least stable aspect of personality and forgets its promises, and in fact has very little tendency in concerning itself about commitments. It can be swayed easily by strong incentives to adopt a different position or role, or just drops an existing one when Ego begins to interfere. When we cannot keep our promise to change, our partner becomes even more furious and takes our apathy as a direct insult and rejection of his/her love. His/her anger reflects how his/her need for love is threatened and thus causing his/her suffering. Our partner perceives the broken promise as a rebellion, retaliation, or loss of love depending on the circumstances.

Overall, we hope love and marriage per se give our partner enough incentive to change. Our egoism and naivety force us misjudge our power and the possibility of making our partner think and act according to our life outlook. We believe that if s/he loved us enough, s/he would change to prove it. We like to test our partner's capability and sincerity in his/her declaration of love and devotion. Thus, we expect her/him to change immediately, often drastically. If s/he does not change, we take it as a sign of inadequacy of her/his love and commitment, if not sudden hostility and rebellion altogether.

Why Cannot We Change?

We cannot really detect and control our Ego easily in order to affect a real change. We may change our attitude but not our essence, which comprises our way of thinking, convictions, habits, preferences, pride, etc. To prove this point, we can refer to experiences when we faced our partner's retaliation for something. We may remember how quickly we reverted to our Ego despite our effort to reflect an 'attitude' change. We got angry, even when Model had meant to keep us tactful, or our Self had meant to be compassionate and understanding of our partner's inherent flaws. This shows that 'attitude change' is often a superficial act with no deep meaning and conviction for the person displaying a change. Meanwhile, our inability to change makes our partner angry and disappointed. S/he concludes that, not only we do not love her/him because the change is not internalized, but also s/he has been fooled all this time by our phony display of change. Thus, relationships deteriorate further by partners' tentative and shallow changes. The only exception is when one partner undertakes such basic changes as steppingstones to explore new avenues, which may eventually lead to self-awareness and essential change over time. Tentative attitude changes are helpful in calming the turbulent situations, but partners must know why change cannot be deep unless it happens gradually through self-awareness, personal conviction, and experience. We should not depend on our partners' fake changes to satiate our 'need for love' or as a measurement of his/her real 'love.' These tentative changes, and their real values and purposes, are unreliable, though they may be useful for stabilizing relationships atmosphere.

An interesting scenario usually occurs after we go through a few rounds of temporary changes without success. In our next round of negotiations for change, we decide and demand that this time we would compromise (change) only if, and only after, our partner has demonstrated authentic changes first. We expect our partner to prove that his/her change is real and permanent before we adopt and show the changes that s/he is expecting from us in return. Interesting and comical enough, hardly anybody agrees with this demand. This scheme (threat) cannot motivate us to change anyway. In a similar scenario, sometimes we do not discuss our demands for change explicitly with our partner, but implicitly contemplate the possibility of changing our attitude in some respects if our partner changes his/hers first in the areas of our desire. All these scenarios demonstrate our high frustration with broken promises, and thus resorting to desperate means of bargaining. These situations, which often sound very much like blackmail and threat, prevail when partners lose their trusts for effecting change.

Promising to change, but more so hoping to convince our partners to change, happens quite often in the early stages of relationships when partners try desperately to save their marriage. On the one hand, the mere intention to change (whether one partner changes first or both partners do it simultaneously) reflects their sincerity and deep desire to make their relationship work. On the other hand, it shows how hollow and naive our promises for change can be and how little we know about the possibilities of change. It also shows our struggles to activate our Model as much as possible to portray a change that we do not believe in truly, or cannot control. Sometimes, partners consent to a mutual change of attitude, while they do not like the demanded changes in principle anyway. They usually call this a compromise. Yet, deep down, they might not be convinced of the value of their efforts. They are only agreeing to change (cooperate) in order to get something they need or merely to calm the situation, but not that they believe change is good for them personally, or even for improving their relationship. The effect of this kind of compromise is discussed in the next section.

The Effects of Demanding Change

Despite partners' inherent resistance to change, often their intention to compromise, for the good of their relationship, over-activate their Model, which then affects the other aspects of their personalities indirectly too. We do this in social and organizational relationships as well as marriage in order to cope with tough situations and accommodate others. Our influence over one another has both positive and negative implications. A positive impact happens mostly when Model strives to show compassion, and maybe overcome Ego eventually, and perhaps even internalize that compassion as a deep 'self' trait. It means that, under this special circumstance, the individual really grasps and believes in the *purpose* of change and practices it with an open mind and heart.

On the negative side, we often begin to resent our partner and marriage even more when playing Model is solely for the sake of stopping our partner's nagging. Increasing our Model requires a comparable reduction of either Ego or Self. Ego is rarely reduced, and it happens *only* when change is internalized in the long run as an accepted target for improving personality. Thus, our integrity and Self is sacrificed most often in the form of lower 'self'-esteem, and 'self'-image, when we continue to play a sharper Model without believing in it as a right attitude or thought. As long as a change is not essential (in our mind), we know that our shallow 'attitude changes' are bound to collapse when we get tired of playing a role, find other priorities, or revert to our real personality and let Ego rule over the Model again—as it normally does and feels more natural too.

Another side effect of using Model is that it must be constantly kept alert, or it would lose its focus and direction. For example, we may inherently nurture a lot of love in our Self, but are unable to express it freely. Therefore, we use our Model to express love as part of a relationship therapy. This therapy makes us attentive on the surface, but the process feels in conflict with our nature and integrity. In addition, after a short while our partner's expectations get used to our new attitude and heightened level of attention to her/him. Our improved attitude gradually feels inadequate to him/her again, and thus s/he makes new demands for even higher attention. If we forget only once to express our love in a particular and timely manner, it would again be conceived as a loss of love.

As another conundrum, marriage partners have taken the position that change proves love and love justifies change. Yet, they mostly want the change in their partner, instead of themselves, at least for becoming less demanding and selfish personally. Accordingly, they impose unnecessary burden on their marriages and communication, and thus increase both partners' level of sufferings in their relationship due to their misperceptions about 'change.'

The rules of relative success in marriage are not hard to discuss, but are difficult to believe in and implement. The first rule is to do not make foolish assumptions about the possibility of change, especially before marriage and during the process of evaluating our partner. Second, often only temporary 'attitude changes' may be expected from 'our demand for change,' at best. Essential changes can only happen from within a person and not through an outside force or someone else's demands. Third, love and being in need of love are different things and neither of them can play a role for change. Only our misunderstanding about the relationship between 'love' and 'change' is causing so much hassle in marital relationships. Fourth, we must focus on changing ourselves to understand and accept the relationships' needs in the difficult environment of the new era. And finally, remember that major causes of conflict in a relationship erupt when a partner tries hard to change the other, knowingly or inadvertently, while the other partner feels pressed to change without being genuinely motivated to change. Why change anyway, when the reason for change does not feel natural. Deep down there is a resistance and inner voice that says, "I do not want to (or cannot) be like you or anybody else." Knowing that change cannot be easy, we can revise our degree of premarital optimism and stop hoping that we can make our partner change. Even worse, we expect marriage by itself make our partner change for the better anyway!

Some interesting suggestions in John Gray's book, *Men are from Mars, Women are from Venus,* might help men and women adjust their attitudes and become more acceptable and pleasing to their partners. On the other hand, the above discussions regarding the instability of 'attitude change' suggest that we need a more fundamental technique to bring partners closer together. We need changes in relationship mechanisms, to induce and encourage sensible and realistic commitments between partners (instead of relying mostly on role-playing to get along superficially, while raising each other's frustration and inner conflicts). We need only one major change in our common mentality: To grasp the role and needs of relationships in the new era. Although men and women seem radically different mentally, they have the same basic need, i.e., for companionship—as their most urgent and essential need. Although men and women might seem to have come from different planets, the only way they can come to harmony and peace is by inventing and understanding a common language. Sometimes, it seems that perhaps women have become homesick due to many years of exploitation by men on the Earth. Therefore, now these two genders have real difficulty understanding each other's language, especially for all the ambiguities that new lifestyles, role-playings, and social values have brought about. For any possibility to resolve the existing marital problems and miscommunications, better relationship guidelines and a common language must be developed. Perhaps we succeed in a couple of centuries or so! That is, if women have not already returned to Venus by then, *which*

*could be one kind of a solution. Or maybe we could send men
back to where they came from!*

The Ultimate Frustration

Eventually couples reach the conclusion that their whims for
changing their partners and building a relationships environment of their liking are futile. They feel defeated and their
frustration appears in their attitude. They try to cope, but cannot stop nagging and blaming their partners for everything,
often without any direct cause for doing so. They do it merely
to relieve themselves from their lingering frustrations and
agonies. Partners lose trust and respect for each other and instead feel spiteful regularly. Their ideas and suggestions usually erupt in hostile tones and their marriage turns into the bat-
tleground for firing blames and nagging at each other.

Partners' blaming and nagging attitude may be either a de-
liberate or an unconscious reaction, but either way, they exhaust partners and their relationship. Ego drives this attitude
with no sign of Model's flexibility to soothe even the elemen-
tary frictions that erupt in any relationship. Naturally, Self is
obviously absent when nagging and blaming goes on. Ordi-
narily, using Model can help in expressing one's sufferings
and needs in a more passionate and convincing manner, hoping at least for some tangible and productive communication
and perhaps some sympathy. However, with nagging and
blaming, we lose the chance of showing our honest feelings,
mainly through Model or Self, to keep the situation under control. In general, blaming and nagging reflect our inner sufferings due to our failure to change or manipulate our partner or
they relate to our unrelenting need for attention.

Partners' frustration and spite also goad their need for controlling and dominating each other somehow. Our urges for
domination of family life and our partner obviously reflect our
inherent frustration for our inability to manipulate our partner.

It reflects our intention to control the decisions, actions, and behaviours of all family members. We need to do this in order to ensure things proceed as we think is best for all. We might even have the good intention of saving the relationship from going the wrong way. However, mainly, we wish to control our destiny and independence as much as possible. When our needs for control and independence are threatened by the objections and interferences of our spouse, we quickly see the need to dominate the situation and our spouse. We do not want surprises, risks, and troubles. We like everything to proceed smoothly as we have planned personally and perhaps with input from our parents or friends. We simply feel a need to control family issues and situations. However, when we find out that our spouse likes to influence those same issues and situations, we are left with no option but to control our partner as well. Thus, the logical tactic in our minds is to control any situation and person that may affect the outcome of our plans and expectations for a kind of life and relationship we prefer. We expect our partner to understand and agree with our values, perceptions of life, and logic. We believe our way of life is the most logical one and thus everybody should agree with it after we explain it to them, often in our crooked language. However, if we cannot come to some agreement, we plan and persist to remain in control somehow, or else we get agitated and retaliatory all the time.

CHAPTER NINE
Life's Hardships

MARRIAGE and divorce cause enough hardships for most people in modern societies. However, other facets of life, including our professions and careers, weaken our spirits, too, which in turn make our job of coping with our marriage conundrums even more difficult. We face too many disappointments due to our unyielding ambitions, people's wickedness, and our rising expectations from the vacant life, *anyway*. Our efforts to figure out life do not seem to lead to any tangible results, either, while deep down our urges to know our purpose of living overwhelm us. With such frantic state of mind, living pressures make our relationship burdens feel too heavy. Thus, we feel trapped on the alienation path quickly, and often rush out to ask for separation and divorce prematurely.

Ironically, we cause many of our own sufferings often for no tangible reasons other than egoism and naïve misperceptions about life, human nature, and relationships' capacity. Instead of staying content with simple stuff, selfless love, and compassion, we pain ourselves in vain by letting our obsessions with fanciful needs and ideologies taint our minds and spirits. In all, our rising expectations in the new era from both life and our relationships have made us impatient and less willing to understand our own faults for causing relationship conundrums and deepening life's hardships.

All these hassles are the symptoms of living in supposedly modern societies that raise our expectations from relationships too much. In recent decades, we have built a complex life structure and crooked social values that cause us too much confusion and frustration. We try to cope and succeed in a competitive, superficial, and showy environment. However, the rigid life structure of modern societies further limits life's low capacity to be meaningful, especially for relating to another person. Meanwhile, the amount of social and personal limitations has grown fast too, and thus we feel trapped, unable to define our life purposes or our identity within this mess.

Our insecurities, erratic psychological needs, and quirks have gotten out of hand, while we try to satiate our superficial needs, adapt, and manipulate others with our egotistical, fake personalities. All along, we only keep piling up more inner conflicts as our ambitions and needs hardly ever get satisfied. Instead, our minds wander rampantly in vain to find a solution for this meaningless and confusing life. Thus, we are increasing our own hardships more every day.

Clearly, our needs and sufferings are usually the cause and effect of one another. Our unsatisfied needs create suffering, and our suffering induces more psychological needs (mostly the need for compassion). Everybody demands a lot of attention nowadays to help him/her through the healing process or at least maintaining a minimal sanity. When we suffer, we *need* something to distract us or somebody to guide us. Alas, people are becoming less capable of filling this void for one another. Therefore, we often end up going out shopping and wasting our time and money on useless stuff!

Our neediness and despair create erratic thoughts, illusions, and pain. Yet only our thoughts (valid reasoning) can contain our needs and insecurities somewhat. Only the right kinds of thoughts can eradicate our sour thoughts and heal our sufferings. Friendships and consoling can mitigate our pains, too, of course. However, ultimately, we must come to terms with our sufferings on our own through rational thinking. Therefore, the bigger irony is that only we can eradicate our life's hardships and suffering with proper thinking. Yet, we only increase our hardships by mundane thoughts and deeds.

Life's hardships compile because we refuse, or do not know how, to review the true reasons behind our suffering, insist on creating foolish justifications for it, or doubt their triviality within the overall scope of our existence. Often, we blame some imaginary causes or find excuses for our suffering and our feeling of self-pity, and perhaps hope to attract other people's sympathy too. All along, we only cause our suffering for no reason other than the weakness of our convictions and souls, and sometimes out of laziness to take proper actions for getting out of our self-imposed mental slump.

Sometimes, we doubt or deny the causes of our suffering and do not admit that our stress is a symptom of a widespread social problem, i.e., the vanity of our lifestyles. We often ignore our inner feelings (conflicts) that signal the real causes of our suffering or quickly turn them into the feelings of defeat, self-pity, and uselessness. Sometimes, we deliberately suppress our thoughts and the symptoms of our hidden problems, e.g., neediness or greed. Sometimes, we allow some elusive concepts like love and happiness deceive our understanding of reality. When we doubt our inner feelings and instincts about our suffering, we do not show any interest or motivation to adjust our approach to life and living. Not knowing our real reasons for living, or adopting erroneous purposes, cause our sufferings too. We are often too stubborn to accept the fact that our shallow mentalities cause our suffering, and instead keep pushing the same values and methods that have proven impractical and stressful. A good example is our absolutely erroneous approach in marital relationships and still continuing with the same methods and expectations. We cause our own sufferings through our idealistic and whimsical thoughts.

Taking Charge of Our Life

Our life struggles have become too overwhelming because we refuse to adjust our expectations, mentalities, and attitudes. And because we refuse to acknowledge the reasons behind our sufferings, which are mostly self-induced—often due to our naivety about the meaning of life. Only we can mitigate our sufferings by learning to ignore those insignificant life events and expectations that trigger our erratic thoughts and break our spirits.

Enough clues are around us about our misunderstanding of life. We must use them for enhancing our self-awareness instead of ignoring them. Our frustration and anxiety often reflect our inattention or misinterpretation of the causes of our suffering. We feel sad because our struggles to overcome our problems seem futile. We feel helpless and lonely because our search for love and happiness only make us more exhausted and stressed out every day. We try to correct the whole world and to make everybody understand our concerns. We like to inform our friends and family about our failing relationships and ne-glected needs. However, it seems, the more we try, the less we succeed to communicate with the rest of the world. Our frus-trations and anxieties keep rising and we look in the wrong places for remedies. Yet we refuse to reassess our value systems and adopt a simpler lifestyle, naively believing we have already figured out the meaning and purpose of life.

Another problem is that we look externally for the causes of, and the cures for, our sufferings. We look for the faults of others, things, and systems. We ignore that mostly our own defects, and our persistence to take the perceived world too seriously, produce our sufferings. Our ignorance of our inner powers inhibits our real potentialities to surface and energize our existence, while our thoughts and primary wisdom also lack a strong foundation. Grasping these concepts is difficult for a person who is trying hard to find an honest job and meet his financial obligations, but keeps failing due to discrimination or job shortages. However, if he finds the wisdom of living in the real world, realizes his inner powers, and looks for his few real needs instead of many superfluous ones, then perhaps he would stop caring too much about finding a job altogether. He learns to create his own job, accept a lower paying job, or maybe even ponder the possibility of living without a job if he has the psychological power and resources to do so. The bottom line is that *ideally* not even joblessness should be a cause for chronic stress and suffering. It must *ideally* induce more creativity to explore other options and opportunities for living.

We must also admit that our personality and psychological flaws create pain and problems for others and us. Personal idiosyncrasies differ according to our unique needs, interests, and willpower. The healing can begin only when we stop doubting the fact that our defects and obsessions are causing most of our sufferings. We must acknowledge our paranoia and hang-ups, and learn how to view, defuse, and cure them. We need the courage and commitment to overcome the main barrier, i.e., our denial of the depth of our insecurities and eccentricities. We have some lingering doubts about our identity and purity, but fail to stop and analyse them.

We must also admit that nobody out there in society is going to change to accommodate us and reduce our sufferings. The chance of finding our soul mate or even a reliable companion is also quite low. The odds would not rise if we keep imagining otherwise or dreaming. We must learn to accept, and live with, all these painful facts of life. Actually, we should expect the matters to get worse and pressures to mount in the years to come. We must accept the hard reality that no one understands and cares about our sufferings and real needs the way our imagination desires. Life hardships would hit us all our lives with very limited, if any, compassion.

The mere acknowledgement of our defects and the causes of our sufferings most likely mitigates the feelings of frustration and helplessness already. The next step is to use this awareness to subdue these known (deep-rooted) causes of sufferings gradually. Only we can adjust our mentality and adopt a more practical life philosophy. We can change our lifestyle and attitude to subdue our sufferings, and maybe even remove our personal defects and desires causing them.

We can build a profound foundation of thoughts upon personal experiences, through studying the visions and prophecies of great thinkers, and by making a finer judgment about the truth of existence. We can weed out the influence of social conditioning on our thoughts and our power of reasoning. We can refute common ideas and perceptions that are senseless. We can resist the temptation of living and thinking for external approval, sexuality, greed, and power—as they are the direct sources of our sufferings. And we can refuse to comply with superfluous standards and expectations propagated in society.

Common Sources of Suffering

Although we have unique personal reasons and remedies for our sufferings, most of them have common sources. Learning about the nature of epidemic social sufferings can heighten our awareness and lead to faster recovery. We can learn to manage our pains and paranoia better by pinpointing the insignificant thoughts behind them. Of course, the nature of suffering and its intensity varies according to individuals' sensitivity, insecurities, weaknesses, surroundings, and outlook on life. Nevertheless, the common sources of mental sufferings relate to some kind of personal needs deprivations, such as:

- Financial burdens and worries
- Social burdens, sexual deprivations, and loneliness
- Paranoia, greed, jealousy, spite, etc
- Psychological defects and chemical reactions in brain
- Lack of social recognition, insecurities
- Personality imbalance due to excessive Ego or Model

- Stress, fears, physical issues, unfulfilled dreams, etc.
- Incomplete or problematic relationships
- Lack of self-actualization and spirituality
- Boredom

Often more than one of the above sources mix and cause niggling thoughts and a feeling of mental suffering. The fact that our sufferings are creations of our thoughts does not mean they are not real. Yet, their intensity is based on our perception (thoughts) about their importance, causes, and effects. Remembering this fact and controlling our thoughts help us mitigate our sufferings, mostly by redefining our purposes of living. Furthermore, solutions are found easier for most of these causes if we unlearn the conventional methods and criteria of assessing our problems. We must become a bit more creative in circumventing social inconveniences and pressures. What we perceive as a problem might not be a real issue at all within a new perspective. Of course, suffering is mostly an emotional reaction, which is hard to measure quantitatively or set a rigid criterion about. Normally, our minds evaluate a recent situation in reference to past experiences or erroneous expectations (as a criterion) to gauge its intensity. Our conditioned brains do some tricky and hasty assessments before we start to feel the suffering. Thus, we must discard the patterns and directions of our conditioned minds, and instead, depend on our awareness to assess the causes and effects of a recent painful experience in a compassionate manner.

We have the option of 'self'-therapy or seeking the assistance of experts to overcome the depression caused by our psychological defects, or Ego and Model. All we need is an initial awareness and honest assessment of our weaknesses, which cause our suffering. We can help ourselves if we really believe that some *adjustments* are necessary. However, most of the time, we really do not see our deficiencies or believe in our ability to overcome them.

Obviously, some sources of sufferings are more difficult to control. This usually happens when brain chemicals and external forces create or reinforce the sufferings. For example, financial burdens are always tangible and possibly due to no fault of our own. Even when caused by our defects such as laziness or extravagance, we still suffer, maybe even more, though at least we could try to do something about it. If we are reasonably aware, and make use, of our potentials to make a living, and do not waste our resources on unnecessary habits or ideas, then our financial hardship is probably not our fault. Or when we have difficulty with our relationships, it is often hard to adjust the situation. In most cases, it is also difficult to get out of them without causing a different kind of suffering for ourselves and others. Still, some alternatives may exist to alleviate the suffering. These kinds of unsolvable relationships can be worked out with some *adjustments* in the foundation of our thoughts and attitude when the situation itself cannot be rectified. Usually couples must find a more practical relationship model to help them interact more productively, even if it would have be a rather passive relationship.

We can choose a personal life path and develop a sensible mentality away from the influence of our lifelong biases and prejudices. A sound foundation of thoughts definitely shows us the need for passion and compassion, flexibility, stability, strengthening our beliefs, grasping 'self,' understanding the true means of happiness, and a life philosophy that inhibits sufferings. During this process, as our wisdom grows, we might gain some insights about life's mysteries, too, which would be only a sacred personal achievement, but never a definite and universal interpretation. Nobody can ever develop a satisfactory meaning for life.

Our sufferings, their causes, and our incessant search for a more peaceful means of living are merely the symptoms of our negligence to strive for self-awareness and the wisdom of a *'self'-control* life. Once we learn to live under the guidance of 'self,' according to the simple rules of the real world, we would not face as much suffering in our highly demanding societies. In the real world beyond our demented illusions about life, our wisdom would be sufficient to void the sources, and avoid the thoughts, of suffering. We would be able to anticipate the situations, thoughts, and feelings of suffering. We may even be able to turn them around to our advantage in the form of passion and compassion, which are usually the main keys for discovering a few basic things about the big mysteries of life.

We can readily grasp and relate to the common sources of sufferings. However, some deep causes of sufferings are due to the deprivation of our inner needs, including spirituality. This happens when we neglect to place sufficient emphasis on significant matters of life and to relinquish the majority of nonsensical desires, ambitions, plans, thoughts, actions, and decisions that we have been emphasizing on uselessly.

A fundamental cause of suffering is loneliness. The impression of loneliness hurts many people all by itself, even if they are only slightly ignored or when they are alone just a few hours. They are simply not prepared to bear even temporary loneliness, or even the impression of it. Obviously, many options exist nowadays for groups or individuals to work together to alleviate their sufferings due to loneliness. However, learning about the positive side of loneliness can reduce our fears of it, too, at least partially. During our no-thought experiences, we learn how moments of solitude (loneliness) could be relaxing and peaceful. Naturally, loneliness on a long-term basis is more complex than occasional ones. However, we can create some no-thought experiences to inhibit loneliness sufferings, learn some self-reliance, and perhaps induce higher consciousness and exceptionally divine feelings.

Drawing upon the sacred energy and passion that a no-thought state or loneliness creates, we can satisfy our deeper needs, which automatically generate tranquility and freedom. In those moments and conditions, we can create beautiful things and thoughts that override the feelings of loneliness many folds. The only problem is that our fears and conventional view of loneliness do not allow us to test and appreciate the advantages of solitude. We have become so desperately attached to things and other people, and, as a result, developed this tremendous paranoia and phobia about loneliness. Yet, in the real world, in fact, we are alone and stay lonely, even if we have a house full of friends and family. This does not mean that socializing is unimportant, but rather to recognize the merits of solitude early on in our lives. A more important point here is that the fear of loneliness can be cured only by discovering the joy of many life experiences that erupt only from loneliness and are extremely beautiful and full of passion.

Sufferings due to boredom relates to the lack of self-fulfilment. It reflects our negligence to find our niche and developing it. We all have some hidden potentials that press us subconsciously to emerge. They demand our attention or else we feel unfulfilled and empty. Exploring and nurturing our potentialities is difficult. However, once developed, they provide a chance for both 'self'-actualization and personal growth, which are the best antidote for sufferings too. These adventures are merely for internal gratification with no other ulterior motives. These experiences fill our lives with joy and creative energy, which would subdue our stress and banal sufferings due to boredom.

If our suffering relates to greed and jealousy, then it should be obvious how we can get rid of it. Why do we continue to look for more of the same things, which we cannot consume in our lifetime anyway, is difficult to grasp. How much wealth and power is enough? We can only ask our Ego! This only shows the absence of a reliable foundation of thoughts to guide our lives.

We can take these steps to develop a solid and sensible mentality away from the influence of our lifelong biases and prejudices. A sound foundation of thoughts shows us the need for passion and compassion, flexibility, stability, strengthening our beliefs, knowing 'self,' understanding the true means of happiness, and a life philosophy that inhibits sufferings.

CHAPTER TEN
Personal Dilemmas

LOVE and loneliness are major life dilemmas for almost everybody, because we seem helpless in choosing a viable option for living and loving. We do not know how to relate effectively, but are not trained to live independently either. Instead, we are fed with all sorts of fantasies about love and filled with the fear of loneliness. Our dependency on social organizations for subsistence and services already jeopardize our self-image, while our financial needs compete with our needs for self-realization and independence. Then, love and companionship needs result in an even higher level of dependence and desperation. In all, a large variety of our conflicting needs create many personal dilemmas for us all our lives.

Right after earning our sense of independence from our parents, we find ourselves in need of loving and being loved. Sexual drives intensify and complicate the matter even further. Therefore, before we really get a chance to test and enjoy our independence, we get drawn into other deep sources of dependence, like love and companionship. We feel our need for dependence even before we actually meet somebody or build a relationship. The mere sense of loneliness and need for companionship weakens our whole image of being and freedom. After we meet somebody and actually start a relationship, the level of dependence increases even more. While trying to cope with, and nurture, our feelings of love and dependence, our inherent need for individualism, as an independent, assertive person, keeps imposing another set of deep inner conflicts. Furthermore, our struggles to distinguish, consciously or sub-consciously, between our love needs and sexual drives become an added source of confusion and doubts.

In all, our desire for independence and our inevitable sub-mission to our urges for love and sex turn into major dilemmas throughout our lives. We struggle all along to solve these dilemmas by fixing (and balancing) our feelings somehow, helplessly and uselessly. While we have more feelings of control and independence during some periods, we soon revert to our need for love and the feelings of dependence that come with it. For either love or sex, or simply eluding loneliness, we have to depend on somebody else who is willing to share similar feelings or experiences with us. Our relationships require mutual dependence and understanding in order to stabilize. Without some degree of commitment and integrity, relationships do not last or take the required form to satisfy our need for a companion. All these requirements create major paradox in our personal lives but also across the society.

Our ceaseless failures to satisfy our need for dependence or independence cause psychological shocks, and lead to depression. For one thing, we start to doubt our identity and 'who we are' without a companion. We doubt our sense of love and companionship and we doubt the effectiveness of our approaches to find and manage them. We start to doubt our ability to judge and decide about our preferences and options on this matter, and about our ability to be an independent person. We get entangled between our emotions and logic fighting forever. On the one hand, our doubts could be a blessing under the circumstance, because our raw logic or emotions could cause even more mayhem, including the risks of forcing hasty decisions. On the other hand, the sense of helplessness in decision-making and our stressful doubts during the perpetual cycles of dependence-independence are not easy to deal with either. These natural, conflicting personal feelings are painful, while we face the rising headaches of relationships in society and couples' inability to relate nowadays despite their deep needs for a reliable companion.

Marriage and companionship are the biggest sources of lingering doubts in life, because both options of living alone and with someone else cause us pain and stress nowadays. Sometimes, loving someone makes us feel even lonelier when we cannot relate to him/her effectively and often feel helpless and unappreciated. This endless source of doubt and stress is a reason why marriage has become a major life decision. Our warranted doubts and cynicism about relationships, and the effects of dependence-independence cycles, reflect the deterio- rating state of relationships and the growing complexity of our basic need for love and companionship. The vast scope of re- lationship issues is best evident from the ongoing frictions and problems in our own or other families and the rising percent- age of marriage failures. In all, the level of deficiencies and deprivations caused by love and loneliness nowadays make the topic of relationships quite sensitive and important for in- dividuals and society as a whole. We are facing the beginning of a major crisis and nobody seems to know how to go about it either. Nobody seems to really care either!

Why Marry?

Our *needs* for sex, love, and compassion are natural motives for getting married. Furthermore, our cultures and ethics de- mand that we engage in some formal ritual to make relation- ships binding and dependable. The purpose of these rules is to protect individuals, enhance family values, and strengthen the nucleus of social structure. All along, we have learned to ex- pect a stable relationship (preferably a marriage) with a person we have spent a lot of time to find and tame. On top of all these natural and cultural motivations, however, nowadays partners have grown high expectations from relationships in line with their rising personal needs and dreams. These new needs, especially partners' craving for love and attention, have risen drastically in recent decades and thus making the task of relating in relationships difficult. People are obsessed to find happiness, which they believe comes mainly from love and *ideal* relationships. However, this is a bizarre expectation—to make our partners responsible for bringing us that illusive happiness that we seem incapable of finding on our own. We ignore the fact that since nobody can find that elusive happiness, expecting it from one another in a relationship is pure silly. The relationship environment has also become too complex as people have become more selfish, greedy, and unreliable. While they seek deep love and lasting relationships, they are losing their sense of commitment to cultural or general family values. No new guidelines exist either to at least provide the basic rules of relating in relationships to keep partners' Egos manageable. So people get into their relationships with crooked motivations and idiotic expectations. While they have become oversensitive and obsessed with finding love, they have little compassion and patience themselves. Under this confusing situation, people settle for a companion for all the wrong reasons without any knowledge of relationship needs or even a true sense of love, though they naively consider 'love' the main success factor for building their relationships. Accordingly, they also get out of their relationships with equally selfish motivations and hasty decisions in pursuit of better companions and more sexuality. People often seem to get married according to their calculating minds and agenda while misperceiving or ignoring the real purposes of relationships.

Overall, it is becoming difficult to assess partners' (often crooked) personal motives for starting a relationship beyond the natural needs of humans (for a companion). Thus, a keen assessment of our motives (both our own and partner's motives) is required before making a decision or committing ourselves to a binding relationship. Obviously, all these doubts and decisions have incredibly high consequences on the quality of our lives, either positively or negatively—mostly negatively, though, in the new era.

Certainly, life is more beautiful and tolerable when the outcome of our decision about a companion is positive and we have a peaceful, pleasant life with a person whom we deeply care for and understand. A compatible and agreeing partner brings the most gratifying experience for a normal person with average intelligence. Conversely, if our decision turns out bad, which seems to be most likely nowadays, the repercussions are often too extensive and destructive. Decisions about marriage normally result in one of these extremes, although some couples learn to live peacefully together despite their conflicts and differences. These facts seem to be obvious and common sense. However, for whatever reasons, most of us fail in our decisions and end up in some form of entrapment. More than fifty percent of marriages in North America lead to divorce. And another great majority of couples live separately or continue living in substandard relationships all their lives with no guts to get out of them.

If we think we are smart when we are making our marriage decision, then why are most of us failing? It seems that we are wrong in our decisions because:

i) We are unaware of the purposes of marriage outside our superficial attraction to another person and our idiotic, high expectations.

ii) We do not analyse, or ignore, our own or our partner's motives.

iii) We do not know enough about relationships' unique needs and the individual we are planning to marry.

iv) We are not familiar with the harsh realities of married life beyond our limited observations of our parents and perhaps some friends or relatives.

v) In fact, we do not even take our parents' experiences seriously, as we think we are immune to their types of mistakes and problems.

Simply, we do not know what we are getting into. More catastrophic, no longer any reliable norms and guidelines exist for partners to use for planning and maintaining their marriage. Meanwhile, their extreme Egos and misperceptions keep increasing their expectations from relationships.

It is interesting how much time and energy we spend on simple decisions, such as buying a pair of shoes. Especially women endure a big dilemma to stay rational, considering their obsession for shoes nowadays. We assess its quality, our need for it, where we are going to wear it to, price, etc. We wish to justify our decision logically (because we have to pay for it) instead of emotionally (simply because we like it). Yet, considering the lifetime consequences of marriage, we do not study the right factors and our motives properly or at all. When it comes to love and sex or the presumed benefits of marriage, we often lose our sense of logic and foresight. We are fooled by the mirage of marriage too prematurely. By the way, humans' long list of obsessions for many things, including shoes, love, or happiness, reveals their inherent irrationality and carelessness in assessing their real needs and purposes. Driven merely by our obsessions for love and happiness, false emotions, or financial incentives, we forget to study the needs and complexity of relationships adequately beforehand. We are not realistic about life anymore.

Considering the magnitude of marriage decision, we have not learned how to define and study the relevant factors of relationships' success. We do not spend nearly enough time to learn and apply proper criteria to measure marriage variables and situations. Heck, we do not even have any guidelines and criteria to use, anyway. Of course, we take a lot of time supposedly thinking and evaluating our options and decisions. However, our hesitations and doubts about marriage or selecting a companion do not necessarily mean that we are studying the matter logically. We are not really aware and informed of the right factors to consider, anyway. Especially during the courting period, we are overwhelmed with many thoughts and emotions that are more distracting than helpful for a true assessment. We usually get swayed by our infatuation and sexual needs; we believe we should compromise; or we ignore or undermine our preferences, purposes, and intentions. We do not give enough weight to the importance of this decision, because we are unaware of the repercussions of bad marriages, which is almost an epidemic nowadays.

Often our motive for marriage is merely a change in our monotonous lives. Sometimes, a partner views marriage merely a means of financial security. In another case, a person lowers his/her standards of an acceptable spouse because s/he is getting old and perhaps her 'biological clock is ticking' too fast. Thus, we jump into a marriage carelessly, hoping that it would work out fine. Both our instincts and need for compassion due to social pressures make us so needy for a partner. Accordingly, our needs for belongingness and love have the strongest mental impact on our daily lives both positively and negatively. They are supposedly medium range needs of humans, but are emerging nowadays quite urgently as deeply psychological attachment needs. Considering the fact that our needs for food and security are somewhat attainable and automatic in modern societies, love and belonging needs occupy our minds and psyches the most all our lives. In that sense, 'search for a companion' manifests as a basic human need, since we all crave it so intensely and passionately and yet often fail to satisfy it properly, if at all.

Finding the right companion makes the biggest impact on our psyches, as it affects our emotions and life outlook permanently. Companionship provides great happiness when it is successful, but it causes extreme pain and disappointment when it is loaded with arguments, failures, and separation. Unfortunately, the latter case is becoming more prevalent. Marriage is certainly a big change, but as statistics indicate, it is usually a change for worse. Therefore, we cannot stop asking, "Why get married in this hectic environment?"

The answer is obvious, of course! Among all our needs, belongingness and love put the biggest pressure on our psyche and we seem unable to stop seeking a companion obsessively. We are just too adventurous and rather realistic perhaps, because finding a right mate has become so challenging.

Epilogue

SOLUTIONS for our marital conflicts are rare and relative. Most of us do not even understand the problems, or make our selfish diagnosis quickly. Yet we should start recognizing the universal problems that inflict most families. They are similar in nature and causation and have become epidemic in the new era. We must believe that miscommunication, incongruity of partners' objectives, high expectations from life and relationships, and our idiosyncrasies play major roles in causing intolerance, misunderstanding, and alienation. We should seriously doubt the possibility of finding a partner even remotely compatible with us, or able to build a relatively quiet life together. Our personal experience would definitely confirm the statistics about all these facts. Accordingly, we must know what kinds of personality adjustments, through the use of Model, are necessary and what kinds of sacrifices we are expected to make just for having a companion.

The health of relationships is surely very important for keeping couples' hardships rather manageable and making relationships somewhat more objective and meaningful again. However, the health of relationships is even more important for maintaining the socioeconomic welfare of any nation. In modern countries, in particular, the deteriorating social condition makes the study of relationships extremely urgent and sensitive, mostly as a *basic* personal need, but also a complex socioeconomic crisis.

Marriage conundrums are deep-rooted and they would continue to soar along with partners' rising expectations, impatience, and intolerance. No remedy seems in sight and not enough research is underway to find a cure. The ideal would be to develop a screening process to at least prevent clearly unfit marriages at the outset. Then, we need an effective process to educate partners initially about the specific needs and hassles of relationships in the new era. We also need substantive therapeutic procedures to help those marriages tainted by destructive germs and viruses. The whole social structure has already been damaged by relationship diseases, as witnessed by disproportionate marriage deaths, and incurable sicknesses. Meanwhile, individuals continue to suffer and live with this epidemic helplessly. The sad fact is that the situation would only get worse in the 21st century. Special attention and commitment by governments to research are needed to change the social and individuals' mentalities about the real purpose of relationships and for finding more practical mechanisms to deal with this matter. So far, governments and legal systems have been only causing more problems than solving relationship conundrums. They are only dealing with the symptoms of this pandemic instead of understanding and curing the roots of the problem. We also need a new approach and mentality about social values that cause such fatal marital diseases.

Couples should spend a few months completing certain educational requirements before rushing into marriage. They should take courses in conflict resolution and negotiation techniques. This may appear contrary to natural laws, but it is no longer the natural laws that determine the marital relationships in modern societies. Marriage has turned into a calculating enterprise and thus need proper contemplation.

And there should be special recognition of individuals who make major contributions in the field of family relationships.

After all, family relationship is the essence and foundation of social life and we are doomed to fail in all fronts if we cannot resolve the problems originated in family nucleus. We have all sorts of prizes for science and literature and even Oscar and Emmy for acting in fictional and superfluous roles. However, we neglect to acknowledge the wisdom and level of tolerance that every individual is extending to act in real life to make a marriage successful. We must honour those who succeed, because a naturally liveable marital life has become scarce. We should give special attention to the development of procedures and cures for marital problems, but also honour couples who can demonstrate their secrets of a successful marriage in a documented way. We need a lot of theory and guidelines to bring objectivity back into relationships. This nucleus of social life needs an overhaul in order to bring back some kind of optimism and positive energy in society. Our random thoughts and sporadic theories about relationships are not enough. A focused approach is needed now. Society must rid itself of the negative effects of marital relationships. We should stop dealing only with the symptoms of relationship failures and instead view the deepening chaos in relationships as a serious social pandemic. There should be a way to get smarter! In particular, the roles of governments and judicial systems should be curtailed drastically. For now, we should 'think divorce at the time of marriage' as a potent precautionary vaccination.